Taxation Simpli

A concise guide to all the basic forms of taxation in the UK. Includes practical down-to-earth descriptions of all the principal areas and methods of taxation, and packed with tips and advice for reducing or avoiding tax. Areas covered include: • income tax • corporation tax • capital allowances • capital gains tax • inheritance tax • value added tax • council tax • self-assessment.

Pensions Simplified

A complete guide to the current pensions system. The book includes a full description of current entitlements under the various types of pension scheme available, both from the State and privately, and gives detailed advice on how to set up a tax-efficient scheme to protect your own future. Areas covered include: • how to choose a pension, set it up and care for it • taking account of the tax implications • retirement planning • what choices are offered at retirement • transfers and opt-outs • dealing with divorce and mortgages • death before and after retirement.

Long-Term Care Simplified

A practical guide to organising and funding long-term care for yourself or a dependent relative. The book includes a full description of the various types of care scheme currently available, both from the State and privately, and gives detailed advice on how to set up a tax-efficient scheme to fund the chosen long-term care plan. Areas covered include: • how to choose the right type of care, at home or in a care home • how to arrange funding for long-term care • what your rights and entitlements are from the State and the NHS • how to protect your property and your assets when providing for long-term care.

Business Protection Simplified

In uncertain economic times it is especially important to take whatever measures you can to protect the profitability of your business. This book covers the whole range of options, including "keyman" insurance, credit insurance, health and safety instruments, currency risk, life assurance, employment insurance, and much more. It also addresses tactical and strategic measures which managers can employ to protect their businesses, through sound financial planning, tax-efficient management, and properly constructed employee incentive schemes.

For further information on any of these books visit www.mb2000.com or telephone Management Books 2000 on 01865 600738

The full list of titles in the "Simplified" series is:

Business Protection Simplified
Inheritance Tax Simplified
Pensions Simplified
School and University Fees Simplified
Succession Planning Simplified
Taxation Simplified
Tax-Efficient Investments Simplified
Tax-Efficient Wills Simplified

For further information on any of these titles,
or for a complete list of Management Books 2000 titles
visit our web-site, **www.mb2000.com**

SUCCESSION PLANNING SIMPLIFIED

Tony Granger

2000

This edition first published in 2013 by Management Books 2000 Ltd
36 Western Road
Oxford, OX1 4LG, UK
Tel: 0044 (0) 1865 600738
E-mail: info@mb2000.com
Web: www.mb2000.com

British Library Cataloguing in Publication Data is available

ISBN 9781852527372

About the Author

Tony Granger has been advising business owners and executives as a business planning specialist and financial planner for more than 25 years. He is responsible for many innovations in the financial planning field to make complicated financial planning concepts easy to understand for both lay and professional reader.

He is the author of many publications and books, including *How to Finance Your Retirement* (Random House/Century), *Wealth Strategies for Your Business* (Random House/Century), *EIS and VCT Investors' Guide* (30 Day Publishing), *Independent Financial Advice and Fee-Based Financial Planning* and the *Retirement Planning Workstation* (30 Day Publishing); *School and University Fees Simplified* (Management Books); *Pensions Simplified* (Management Books), *Inheritance Tax Simplified* (Management Books 2000), *Business Protection Simplified* (Management Books 2000), *Tax Efficient Investments Simplified* (Management Books 2000) and manuals on Trust Administration and Trustees' Duties and Responsibilities.

Tony is a member of the Institute of Financial Planning and holds the CFP^{cm} (South Africa and the United Kingdom), the certified financial planner certificate, as well as degrees in law and commerce. He is a past President of the Institute of Life and Pensions Advisers (Financial Planning Institute) of South Africa, and a member of the Personal Finance Society (PFS), and past President of the Chartered Insurance Institute (Shropshire and Mid-Wales). He lectures regularly to accountants and solicitors, as well as independent financial advisers on a wide range of issues. Tony is visiting professor at the Business School of London Metropolitan University.

Succession Planning Simplified is aimed at consumers and financial advisers alike, and is most topical as people decide on their own future retirement and post-death strategies; trustees make decisions to begin and end trusts; and business owners prepare to develop and then exit the business successfully. There is a planned way to do things that will save time and costs in the long run, and early preparation is key. Leaving matters to chance could end up with your objectives not being met, or at worst tax and other costs that could have been avoided.

Acknowledgements

For proposing this book in the first place, Nick Dale-Harris of Management Books 2000. Nick is a tireless campaigner for easy to read and understand consumer-facing books that make a difference. His meticulous editing and book construction certainly make a difference. To the many IFAs, accountants, solicitors and business owners who have encouraged a sequel to Business Protection Simplified, their support is acknowledged.

Contents

About the Author 5

Acknowledgements 6

Forewords 13

Introduction... 15

Part 1. Succession Planning for Individuals........................... 17

1   Succession Planning in the Event of Your Death 21
    Death planning.. 21
    Wills 22
    Intestacy... 22
    Decision tree – wills 23
    Trusts 25

2   Living Wills 27

3   Estate Planning... 28
    Threats in the estate planning process.................................. 29
    Starting the process 31
    The nil rate band 32
    Bank accounts 32
    Ownership of the house 33

4   Long Term Care... 34

5   Retirement Planning... 36
    Death before retirement 36
    Death after retirement 37
    Occupational pension scheme.. 37
    Money purchase pension scheme 38
    Drawdown schemes.. 38
    Inheritance tax on pension funds... 39
    Ill health and early retirement... 39
    Investments and savings 39
    Your house.. 39

6   Health, Disability and income protection 41

7   Succession Planning and Divorce 42
   Civil partnerships 43
   Ongoing commitments 43
   The house 43
   Remarriage 44
   Separation 44
   Co-habitees 44
   Key points summary 44

Part 2. Business Succession Planning 45

8   Creating the Succession Plan 49
   Set your objectives 49

9   Create a Business Plan 52
   Business plan components 52

10 Identify Possible Exit Routes 54
   Exit routes where the company as a whole is sold 55
   Exit routes – where a partial sale of shares is made 56
   Non- company exit routes 57
   Setting a time line 57

11 Valuing the Business 59
   Net asset value method 60
   Rate of return method/cash flows 61
   Intrinsic value method 62
   Super-profits method 62
   Why you need a valuation? 62

12 Negotiating the Best Price 63
   How to calculate profits for valuation purposes 63
   Increasing business value 64
   The business value formula 64

13 Learning the Numbers 68
   Profit margins 68
   Return on total assets 68
   Return on owner's equity 69
   Learn the important ratios for investors 70

14 Identifying Successors 72
   Career paths 73
   Create a roadmap of future leaders 73
   The drivers in the business 74

Differentiate between leadership and management 74
Investing in the business's talent 75
Implementing a successful succession plan 75
Succession planning as a main strategy.. 76
Who is involved in the succession planning process? 77

15 Critical Influences for Succession Planning.................................. 79

16 Protecting the Business Whilst Building Value.............................. 81
Business risk areas.. 81
Loss of a key person risk 82
Insuring the key person.. 84
Selecting the right kind of life policy.. 85
Make your key person policy tax deductible 85
Policy proceeds.. 85
To ensure premiums are tax deductible, get it in writing from HMRC.... 86
Cost of term (life) cover at various ages and terms 86
Critical illness protection cover 86
Income Protection 87

17 Protecting the Business Owners and Future Heirs......................... 88
Ensure you have key person cover... 89
Develop your succession planning objectives 89
If a sole trader, insure for estate liquidity 89
If a sole trader, have a buy-and-sell agreement with another sole
   proprietor.. 90
If shareholders or partners /LLP members then consider a 'double
   option' agreement.. 90
Examine existing buy-and-sell agreements 90
Check types of life cover and other forms of cover.............................. 91
For maximum flexibility, include Key person cover above the line with
   Shareholder or Partner cover... 91
Holding policies in trust 93
Include employee share scheme trusts, employees and managers
   in your succession planning 93
Enterprise Management Incentive scheme (EMI).................................... 94

18 Using Employees in the Business 95
Employees helping the business sale.. 96

19 Retiring From the Business 97
The succession business plan for retirement...................................... 97
If you do not have a pension scheme 98
Steps in the review process.. 99

Companies... 100
Partnerships and LLP members.. 101
Sole traders.. 103
Continuing liabilities 103

20 **Tax Planning**... 105
Sale of the business.. 105
Planning areas 107
Exiting the business – on death 108
Death – sole trader 108
Partnership or LLP... 109
Companies and shareholders 110
Investing the proceeds... 110
Tax reducing investments 111
Pension contributions as investments.. 111
Tax free investments.. 112
Tax deferred investments.. 112
Investment bonds... 113
Deposit accounts with deferred interest... 113
Capital gains investments 113
Making use of your allowances – taxable investments 114

21 **Funding the Business Exit**... 115
For companies 115
If a partnership or LLP... 116
If a sole trader 116

22 **Exiting the Business Successfully** 118
Succession planning linked to business exits 118

Part 3. Wealth Creation 121

23 **Using the Business for Wealth Creation** 123
Understand the business cycle of profits 124
Your goals for building wealth through the business......................... 124

24 **Profit Strategies for Sole Traders**... 127
Make maximum use of business deductions, allowable expenses
     and capital allowances 127
Introduce your spouse or civil partner or partner, or the family
     members, into the business 127
Increase pension funding to further reduce taxation and build wealth ... 128
Make full use of personal investment and other tax deductions 128
Invest (profits) after-tax income wisely to build up personal wealth 129

25 Profit Strategies for Partners and LLP Members............................ 130
*Reorganise partnership and LLP borrowings to get maximum relief
on interest payments*... 130
*Organise tax planning around partnership/LLP capital accounts to
maximise and preserve wealth*.. 130
Tax planning around partnership losses to preserve partners' wealth.... 132
If you contributed too much partnership capital, get paid interest........ 132
*Make sure that excess allowances over tax due on partnership
share is set off against other income*............................... 132
*Maximise pension contributions as repayment of capital accounts
may be slow* 133
Pay unfunded pensions and cash lump sums to retiring partners 133
Build up an investment fund to pay out capital accounts or pensions.... 134

26 Profit Strategies for Companies 135
Paying dividends or bonuses – decide which is the best route............ 135
*Improve the position of the director by making a pre-tax pension
contribution for him*... 138
Make use of other NIC avoidance schemes to reduce taxation........... 138
*Take out investigation insurance policies if utilising avoidance
schemes*.. 138
Utilise all personal allowances and reliefs to reduce taxes................. 138
*Make sure the business is deducting all it can in capital allowances
and business expenditures*.. 138
Borrow from a director's pension fund rather than a bank.................. 139
Invest retained profits wisely... 139
Sell shares and retain wealth by using capital gains tax exemptions .. 139
Investments and tax shelters 139
*Determine the investment policy of the business and its attitude to
risk*.. 140
Determine the availability of investment resources............................ 141
Determine the future expenditure of the business and its sources 142
Determine the best investment 142
*Select the most tax-efficient investments for surplus cash and invest
in tax shelters* 142
*Your best tax shelter is the business's pension fund. Maximise
contributions to it* 143
Use a pension scheme to protect the assets of the business.............. 143
*The company or business may invest in other tax efficient investments
such as EZTs*.. 144
*A company may invest in an ESOT – an Employee Share Owner Trust,
for tax shelter and working capital enhancements* 144
*The business can make investments (usually in property, plant and
machinery) for capital allowances* 145

Invest in legitimate NIC avoidance schemes to build executive wealth . *145*
Get the best interest rates *145*
Pay the best interest rates for loan account money *146*
Review investment arrangements regularly – at least once a year *146*
Help employees to build personal wealth. The 'knock-on' effect
  makes for wealthier businesses *147*

Part 4. Bringing your Succession Planning Strategies together **149**

27 Conclusion **151**
  The ultimate objective *152*

Abbreviations **153**

Bibliography **155**

Index **157**

Forewords

Once again I am pleased to support Tony Granger, in writing this book on *Succession Planning Simplified*. There are too few comprehensive books on business financial planning available in the UK, that are both instructive and useful to business owners and financial planners alike, and this is a must for any corporate financial planner to understand the business and personal succession and exit strategies facing millions of business owners in the short and long term.

Nick Cann, CEO of the Institute of Financial Planning

I don't believe there has ever been the need for a more timely reminder about succession planning and Tony's new publication *Succession Planning Simplified* helps business leaders to implement a plan rather than letting circumstances rule the situation. Tony Granger writes from a practical business owner perspective and this book has taken all variables into account enabling us to make the right succession plan to protect the business and stakeholders' future.

Bob Battye, Chairman of Vistage Groups and Business Coach to CEOs and MDs

Introduction

There is no one definition of succession planning. Most people will be aware of it in a business sense to identify successors to transfer power and control.
A general definition would take into account the following factors:

- Succession planning is a process. It provides for the replacement of one by another.
- It takes into account the future and anticipates likely changes.
- It identifies successors and provides for a smooth transition.
- Decisions are made in advance to cover likely contingencies, without the loss of effectiveness.
- It provides for continuity, and to carry out your wishes, which may include the disposal of your wealth in an orderly manner.
- The preparation of a plan of administration and disposition.
- The succession plan sets out the factors to be taken into account and the process to be followed to replace someone or something, following a major event.

Succession Planning Simplified is timely in that it brings together different strands of financial planning that affect people in planning for their future and how best to consider their savings up to retirement and beyond; the impact of death on a family, taking into account to whom and how to leave your assets; wills (or the lack of one), inheritance taxes and family planning issues; as well as disability, poor health and divorce. Close on 700,000 people retire every year in the United Kingdom, and over half a million die. Most don't do it very well. There were 484,000 deaths registered in England and Wales in 2011 (the third year in a row under 500,000, and falling), of which 238,000 were male and 246,000 female. The 2011 Census revealed that there were 10.3 million people age 65 and over in the UK, projected to increase to 12.7 million by 2018. By 2035 there are projected to be 4 million more people aged 65+ than those aged under 16 (Office National Statistics 2012). The number of people aged over 90 rose by more than 25% to 430,000 in the 10 years since the last Census, and there are three times more women over age 90 than men.

In 2010/2011 in England and Wales there were 119,589 divorces, up by 4.9% on the previous year. The number of divorces in Scotland fell to a 30 year low. The average age for divorcing partners was 44.2 years for men and 41,7 years for women.

People need to plan for many life events. These include divorce, retirement, death, providing for long-term care; providing for their families and loved ones; ensuring they have enough to live on – as they live longer.

How to prepare your *business* for your eventual exit, and how successful that will be, taking into account identifying those who will succeed you and provide leadership for many years to come, are topical planning areas. There are around 5 million businesses in the UK – most are owner-managed, with 10 employees or less. However, their success or failure affects not only the business owner and his family, but also employees and their families. Succession planning is not only about the success of the business – it can also be part of a business failure, and what to do next.

No one knows exactly how many **trusts** there are in the UK. Some are dormant, a trust in name only, waiting to be started on the happening of some event, such as the death of a testator. Examples are 'nil rate band trusts', or life assurance policies in trust – they will only activate once funded. Others are active, and set up for many different reasons, including the protection of immature beneficiaries, such as a spouse unable to deal with money, or minor children. Many are UK based, others reside offshore. It is estimated that there is over £20 billion in trust assets in UK discretionary and interest in possession trusts alone. New trust legislation means that trusts must be regularly reviewed, as many are now hopelessly tax inefficient. Trusts are used as an advanced form of succession planning – yet many are old, out of date and not fit for purpose.

Trusts are also wrapped around pension schemes, and there are also now thousands of child trust funds, as well as trusts set up for purely charitable purposes.

Trust planning is big business and trusts are used for many purposes for individuals as well as businesses.

The author aims to give the reader workable succession planning strategies. For most, these will be broad brush, with outline proposals, for others, a more in-depth analysis is given.

This book is based on our understanding of current tax law and relevant legislation as at October 2013. Please always seek expert advice when contemplating strategies mentioned as circumstances can change and not always be appropriate for you. Where investments are mentioned, values can rise and fall and you may lose your capital. Past performance is no guarantee of future success. Where loans are secured against property, there is always the risk of losing the property where loan repayments are not maintained. Carefully consider your personal circumstances and those of the business before implementing any strategies as the authors, and publisher cannot be held responsible for any acts, errors and omissions (E & OE). Figures used in calculations refer to the 2013/14 tax year (unless as stated otherwise).

Part 1

Succession Planning for Individuals

In the context of individuals, succession planning is the process employed to identify life changing events and then to take decisions on how to plan for these now and how to deal with them in the future. It lays out a decision tree on what your wishes are, as well as your aims and objectives. It is wider in application than merely preparing for death as the sole event to be concerned with. It could relate to retirement, or incapacity for example. First you must decide who will be involved in the succession planning process. Will it be just you, making decisions on your own? Will you involve family members, as whatever you plan for, will affect them? Do you need to consult with professional advisers, such as an independent financial adviser, solicitor or accountant?

The major life events are death, retirement, disability or ill-health.

1

Succession Planning in the Event of Your Death

Death planning

Death planning is about providing continuity for your estate to pass to your selected heirs, on the one hand, and tidying up your affairs on the other hand.

Checklist

- Wills completed and valid. Where is the will lodged/ held?
- Names and addresses of beneficiaries, heirs.
- Letter of wishes to supplement the will – what would you like to happen? (this is for guidance only).
- Is Life assurance adequate and in trust? Try to move policies not in trust to trust, if possible. Policies in trust are not subject to IHT and the proceeds are available before probate.
- Debts and liabilities covered.
- Assets and liabilities listed.
- Investments listed.
- Pensions listed.
- Pensions' nomination form completed. Some may be out of date if divorced, or remarried.
- Use of pensions trust for death benefits to bypass estate for IHT purposes.
- List of names and addresses of solicitor, accountant, IFA, banks and building societies.
- Bank accounts – single and joint names.
- Address of tax office.
- List of gifts and donations made, to whom and when.
- Completion of 'normal expenditure out of income' form, annually (if you have made gifts out of surplus to normal expenditure).
- Use of nil rate band recorded if gifts made, dates and recipients of gift.
- If a spouse has died before you, details of the nil rate band used, or not used.
- If a spouse died and you have remarried – details of previous spouse's nil rate band.
- If divorced – any divorce or court order that may be relevant.

- Details of any trust, especially if you have been receiving income from it as a life tenant.
- A file with your car, household and other insurances.
- If you have accidental death policies (for example some credit cards offer this free) make a note of these.
- If a business owner or shareholder, details of the business ownership and who to contact.
- Doctors and medical advisers.
- Funeral arrangements – do you wish to be buried or cremated? If leaving organs to science, is there an immediate process in place to ensure this happens?
- You can add to this check list any matters that are within your personal circumstances.

Wills

How well have you prepared for your death? It can, of course, happen at any time. It is estimated in the UK today that less than 50% of the adult population have wills. Your will is the document that directs your wishes and dispositions, and sets up any trusts to protect minor or vulnerable beneficiaries.

If you do not have a will, then the rules of intestacy apply.

Intestacy

The rules of intestacy in England and Wales are as follows: (there are variations for Scotland and Northern Ireland).

Assuming the person dies, and after the payment of funeral expenses, tax and other debts owed by the deceased, the rest of the estate will devolve as follows: (note that children includes children born in or out of wedlock and legally adopted children, but not step-children.)

- Leaves a spouse or civil partner, no children or parents or brothers or sisters of the whole blood – then everything goes to the spouse or civil partner.
- Leaves a spouse or civil partner and children.
  - Net estate up to £250,000 – everything to spouse or civil partner.
  - Net estate over £250,000 – the first £250,000 plus personal possessions to the spouse/civil partner. Half the rest is shared equally amongst the children. The spouse/civil partner gets the income or interest on the other half during his or her lifetime, and on death the capital goes to the deceased's children equally.
- Leaves a spouse/civil partner and no children, and either parents, or brothers and sisters of the whole blood:

- – Where the net estate is not more than £450,000, everything to spouse or civil partner.
- – Where the net estate is over £450,000, then £450,000 plus half the rest, plus personal possessions to the spouse/civil partner.
- – The other half to the deceased's parents equally; if no parents, then to brothers and sisters of the whole blood in equal shares.
- If the deceased left children, but no spouse or civil partner: everything to children in equal shares.
- If the deceased leaves no spouse or issue, the estate will pass to the deceased's parents. If neither parent is alive, the deceased's nearest relatives will inherit. The order of priority is as follows:
  a. Brothers and sisters, of the whole blood and the issue of any who have predeceased.
  b. Half-brothers and half-sisters and the issue of any who have predeceased.
  c. Grandparents.
  d. Aunts and uncles (being brothers and sisters of the whole blood of a parent of the intestate) and the issue of any who have predeceased.
  e. Half-brothers and half-sisters of the deceased's parents and the issue of any deceased half-uncle or half-aunt.
- If no living beneficiary, the deceased's estate will pass to the Crown, the Duchy of Lancaster or the Duchy of Cornwall

If not married, and you have no will, then the rules of intestacy apply. Your long term partner could get nothing. A recent law commission report undertaken to consider the plight of unmarried co-habitees, is recommending that co-habitees be treated on a similar basis to those who are married.

Unless your succession plan specifically wishes to include unheard of uncles and aunts, and even the Duchy of Cornwall, then you are strongly recommended to make a will as the first part of your succession plan.

Decision tree – wills

- Draw up a list of assets and liabilities, so that you know what you can leave to others.
- Draw up a list of whom you wish to benefit from your estate.
- If likely to have more children, include unborn children.
- If minors are involved, do not forget trusts to hold their cash and other assets.
- Think about a guardian for your children (if both parents die) if minors. Do not consider parents or grandparents, if possible (unless they have a wish to do so). Ask the proposed guardian if they will be prepared to be a guardian.

- Check your life assurance. Is it in trust? (If not, the life policy proceeds could be liable to inheritance taxes at 40%). Is it enough? A rule of thumb is that if you wish to give your spouse or partner an income on your death and you do not have other income-producing assets or pensions, then decide on a post-death income. If this is say £25,000 p.a. then a lump sum required, if invested at say 5%, would be £500,000. That would be the amount of life cover you need. If you have still to pay off a mortgage, add this to the life cover requirement. If unable to get life cover, your planning will be different.
- If you have a spouse or civil partner, then any assets you leave to them will be completely free of inheritance tax. If not, then the nil rate band for inheritance tax will apply (currently £325,000 in 2013/14 to 2014/15 is free of inheritance tax) to whomsoever you leave your estate who is not a spouse or civil partner. This includes assets left to your children. The transferability of the allowance gives £650,000 to a married couple or civil partners.
- Speak to your solicitor or financial planner about will trusts. These are valuable to protect minor beneficiaries, or a spouse unable to deal with financial management; and for inheritance tax purposes can be used to pass assets to future generations free of inheritance tax. It also enables you to set up controls around your money and assets. For example, remarriage of a spouse, or divorce of a child who inherits from you.

I am often asked questions about where to have a will done, or whether a will form from Staples or Smith's is just as good. You can do it yourself with pro forma wills (costs around £10), however, the cheap version may miss something, and you may be better off taking advice. The average solicitor charges around £120 to £150 for a set of mirror wills (one for you and one for your spouse or partner) if substantially the same. More complicated wills will be more expensive.

Part of your wills succession planning will be to decide who you choose to administer and execute your estate. Usually this is your spouse or partner, but you may wish to add a solicitor or third parties, such as your accountant, or adult children. Again, the issue of charges and fees arise on the administration or gaining probate for your estate. Get this sorted before your death, if possible.

The drawing up of your will should sharpen your perspective in respect of your planning.

However, the will is actually at the *end* of the financial and estate planning process, and not the beginning of it. You should first have a financial plan completed for you to determine a number of issues – and these include which assets are dutiable in your estate (and which are not), and whether you have enough cash in your estate to satisfy your objectives. Many deceased estates comprise property such as the family home which cannot be sold and turned into immediate cash, or investments that you may not wish to sell at the time as the timing may not be right.

Many a personal succession plan has started out on the right foot, only to be scuppered at the final hurdle because the underlying planning was not done first. For example, it is no good leaving in your will £100,000 to each of your three children in trust (£300,000), and £500,000 to your spouse in trust to give her an income of £25,000 per year, plus £200,000 in trust for your elderly parents' care fees costs (a total of £1 million), if your assets comprise your house worth £450,000, ISAs of £50,000 and company shares worth £1 million at your death.

On paper you are worth £1.5 million. However, as there was no succession planning in your business, your company shares are only worth £200,000 on your death, and can't be turned into cash. So, the only cash available is your ISA pot of £50,000 (as your family has to live somewhere, the house is not available as an asset to be turned into cash). The net result is that your children and parents can forget their proposed inheritance, as can your spouse. There simply isn't enough available cash or assets for everyone.

Proper planning could have saved this family's inheritance. The main ingredient for any estate is to have sufficient cash or estate liquidity to enable your objectives to be fulfilled. The business could have affected a key person life policy on your life to enable your shares to have a value, at insignificant cost to the benefits provided, for example, or arranged for your shares to be purchased through a double option agreement with life cover, directing cash to your estate, where it is most needed.

Trusts

Most people are familiar with trusts, as their wills often contain a trust clause to enable funds to be held and protected for future generations, or for minors or immature beneficiaries.

Life assurance policies should be written in trust. The reason for this is that the policy proceeds are immediately available – before probate- and are not subject to inheritance tax on your death if the policy is written in trust. If you have policies not in trust at present then ask your financial adviser to arrange for them to go into trust. It may save you thousands of pounds in the long run.

Some trusts are set up whilst you are alive, and others come into force on your death, or the happening of a certain event.

For trusts set up whilst alive, a gift is made to trust by the settlor (the person who establishes the trust), for the benefit of beneficiaries (usually a spouse or children, relatives or third parties). If a beneficiary is entitled to an income from the trust, he or she is known as a life tenant; those who receive the capital from the trust are known as remaindermen. Trustees are appointed to manage the affairs of the trust, and are governed by the Trustee

Act 2000, which applies to all trusts. If the trustees are in the UK, the trust is an onshore trust. If the trustees are outside the UK, then the trust itself is domiciled offshore, or outside the UK. Common trusts are discretionary trusts (where the trustees have full discretion on acting with regard to investments, payments to beneficiaries and other matters), bare trusts (set up for a minor who becomes absolutely entitled to the trust assets at age 18), or interest in possession trusts, where a life interest is payable to a life tenant.

If the trust gift is below the nil rate band (currently an exempt allowance of £325,000 in 2013/14 which is frozen at this level until 2014/15), then no inheritance tax in advance is payable. If the gift is above this amount then the amount above the nil rate band is subject to inheritance tax at 20%. This is the lifetime rate and is half the death rate of 40%.

For trusts set up on death, these are commonly known as will trusts. They could be bare trusts, interest in possession trusts, or discretionary trusts. They only come into effect on the death of the testator (the person making the will). A trust could also be established on intestacy, without a will, and these trusts are usually statutory trusts.

Every trust also has a nil rate band. Every seven years, you could set up a new trust, also with a nil rate band, which is in addition to the other trusts you have established.

Trusts are useful for succession planning in that they can be used to: (some of the more common usages)

1. Provide for heirs and beneficiaries named or not named.
2. Provide income for a spouse or civil partner, with protections, and capital for the children or grandchildren on the death of the spouse taking the income.
3. To bypass someone who has no need of the trust assets, and to funnel value to the next generation. Often a spouse bypass trust is set up to direct assets directly to the children or grandchildren, for example.
4. To provide for the physically disabled or mentally handicapped.
5. To hold business shares or assets, including life assurance proceeds on the death of a shareholder or partner (business trust).
6. For beneficiaries who are minors, until they reach a certain age.
7. To protect assets on divorce, and insolvency/bankruptcy.

Wills and Trusts are important components of personal as well as business succession planning. The establisher can direct through wishes (letter of wishes for trustees) or instruction (in your will) which assets will go where and when.

2

Living Wills

All adults in England and Wales who are mentally competent can refuse medical treatment either at the time or in advance (apart from medical health interventions). A living will allows you to do this in advance. All adults can make a living will (age over 18 in England and Wales), but if mentally incapacitated, you cannot make one.

Advance Decisions are legally enforceable under the Mental Capacity Act 2005. Health professionals looking after you must follow them. In Scotland, Advance Directives are not legally enforceable under the Adults with Incapacity (Scotland) Act 2000. Health professionals can consider your wishes though. If aged over 16, you can appoint an attorney to take welfare decisions on your behalf if you lose your mental capacity. A Continuing Power of Attorney is used in Scotland. In Northern Ireland nobody can agree to or refuse medical treatment on behalf of another.

You cannot use an Advance Decision to ask for anything illegal to be carried out; nor demand that you are not given food or drink by mouth; nor to refuse basic care.

Living wills should be witnessed and should include your details and also those of your GP and other health professionals and carers. Ask them to note the existence of the Living Will in their files so that if your health and mental faculties deteriorate, there is a record of what you have done. If you change your mind, make sure that this is also recorded. If mentally incompetent later, then your wishes as set out in the Living Will would stand.

If you make a living will before a lasting power of attorney (LPA), then the LPA takes precedence. If the living will is made after the LPA then it takes precedence.

3

Estate Planning

The issues in estate planning are broadly the following:

- Protecting and preserving wealth for yourself, your dependants and future generations.
- Dealing with inheritance and other taxes on your death and the death of a spouse or civil partner, or cohabiting partner.
- Not having to pay IHT upfront, if it can be avoided. Certain lifetime gifts made over the NRB, to a discretionary trust, for example, suffers IHT at half the rate, 20% currently.
- General tax mitigation, reduction, provision for tax to be paid.
- Protect beneficiaries who are young, profligate, immature, financially unable to deal with money, the disabled.
- Providing sufficient income and capital for yourself and your dependants when no longer working or retired, or going into long-term care.
- Medical and other expenditures and costs to be provided for.
- Emigrating abroad – before and at retirement.
- Whether to set up trusts whilst alive or on death. The costs of doing so and whether they are indeed necessary or not.
- Asset allocation and investments taking into account attitude to risk and what the investments are for.
- Changing existing investments to 'wrap' them for IHT protection, and what is involved in the process.
- Staying in the family home or passing it on to the children; losing the home if going into long-term care; equity release issues to provide for usable capital and increasing income and the implications of doing so. Making the right choices for equity release is a major issue.
- How best to deal with business assets and succession planning.
- If farming, how to deal with a small farm and many dependants to be viable.
- Who should inherit from you? Do you leave inheritances to your parents? Your children? Your grandchildren? How much to leave and whether to be equitable or not. One or more children may have had support during your lifetime, others not.
- Leaving money to charity or political parties.
- What to put into your will and what to leave out. The whole issue of executors and administrators and trustees, how they get paid and how

competent are they in dealing with your affairs. Who will advise on bereavement issues?
* Who will advise your heirs after you have gone? Will they be competent? What happens after you die, and what are the processes involved? How up to date must your current personal book-keeping be?
* Once a course of action has been chosen, can it be changed?
* Costs involved in estate planning and who does it?
* What more can you do to ensure a successful outcome?
* What if the laws change and I am too old to deal with new issues?
* The above are very real concerns and have to be dealt with at some time – otherwise they remain largely unanswered questions. They affect those with substantial assets, as well as those with next to nothing.
* The discerning financial planner should guide you through the above check-list in helping you with your estate and general financial planning. It's not just about saving taxes, it is about preparing yourself throughout life to make the best decisions and choices. The more you know, the better prepared you can be.

Threats in the estate planning process

Be aware of the following when doing your planning:

* Investments and savings can rise and fall, depending how and where you have invested. Your risk profile for investments is crucial, as is the amount available for investment. Can you afford to lose capital through taking on particular investment strategies? What is the purpose of your investment? If it is to grow for the next twenty years and then to provide an income, try to avoid an investment that can be eroded by inflation. Inflation is currently in the range of 3-4% per annum, and to make a 'real return' you need to be in inflation-beating investments. How well diversified are you? If one particular class of investment falls, will another type compensate by rising? Asset allocation amongst investment classes is key to diversified performance expectation.
* Not having enough cash (liquidity) in your estate to provide for your wishes. Those without a strong investment base will consider alternatives such as life assurance to provide cash on death. You may wish to fund trusts and to provide for paying taxes without having to sell assets to do so.
* Having incompetent advisers can be a major threat. They may not have the whole picture, or may sell you unsuitable investments. They may not ensure that the correct protections are in place. As many as 70% of new clients seen by me do not have existing life policies in trust, which is a prime example. A simple trust form means that life assurance escapes both probate and IHT. Policies can be written into trust after being taken out, generating substantial IHT savings. Even today, only 30% of policies

that should be in trust are written into trust.

- Unsuitable products and trusts either in existence or affected by new legislation can put your financial planning at risk.
- Changes in financial circumstances making prior planning obsolete. For example, your son is a successful businessman with a substantial estate. Assets you leave him on death will make his estate taxable, and he may not have planned for this- his existing planning does not take into account what you may do. In these circumstances, family estate planning is important.
- Changes in legislation affecting existing planning. Some legislation is retrospective, although there may be a transition period to get things right. For example, in 2006 the Chancellor changed the basis of taxation for interest in possession and accumulation and maintenance trusts. Largely used in will trusts to give a spouse an income from trust assets (interest in possession), that interest was previously not taxable on the spouse's death, but has been after 2008; for accumulation and maintenance trusts, a child could receive income to age 25 and then capital – now the age limit has dropped to age 18 – above that age there are tax consequences. You may not wish a child to inherit at age 18, and may need another course of action or changes to be made to a trust to reduce the incidence of trust taxation.
- Future changes in legislation could be made that affect existing planning. For example, the Government may make PETs taxable (at present you can make a gift to anyone and the value of the gift and the growth on it would be out of your estate after 7 years); business property relief is given up to 100% on qualifying business assets such as private company shares; and up to 50% on certain farm assets from your estate – there is no certainty that these exemptions from IHT will always be there.
- Changes in the tax treatment of financial products that have current legislated-for tax advantages may be removed in the future. There again, a new Chancellor may be more generous, but this is considered unlikely, as the Exchequer can expect around £2.9bn+ from IHT in 2013.
- Not having a financial plan that deals with your issues will be a major threat to your financial well-being, as well as for the well-being of those who succeed you.

The current economic and socio environment is not for the reduction of IHT, nor the preservation of your carefully built-up assets over your lifetime, nor the safeguarding of your families in the long term; nor the preservation of your pension assets for the use of future generations and your dependants; there is no protection of the family home and future financial stability for your dependants; the only thing you can be fairly certain of going forward is an increase in life expectancy; falling pension provision from the State and employers; increased council taxes, income taxes, trust taxes; increasing costs of medical care, to mention a few.

Successful Estate Planning is where you take control, plan as best you can under current circumstances, and make sure that you use the best available financial planning mechanisms to level the playing field.

The Government tax-take will continue to increase largely through inertia. That means you will have done nothing about it, and accept the present position. Believe it or not, but there remain very advantageous procedures that can be undertaken to reduce your estate liabilities, including IHT, and they all quite legal and legislated for. In the same way that your car needs an MOT every year, or you would have a medical check-up from time to time, you also need to engage in a financial plan or have your present planning checked. The benefits are there to be claimed by you.

Starting the process

The following are the steps in the financial planning and estate planning process:

1. Complete a statement of your goals and objectives for yourself at the present time; then project forward how you see the position at retirement; after retirement and on death. What do you see as the result of your planning? You need to do this because if you don't know where you are going or intend to go, it is almost impossible to measure your journey milestones. You can be as general or specific as you wish – it's your plan.
2. Decide how far ahead you wish to plan for. Will planning be for you, your spouse or partner, your children, your grandchildren, and even more future generations?
3. Consider your need requirements now, at retirement, and after your death (for your dependants).
4. Prioritise your objectives and need requirements in order of importance to you. I find it useful to use a scale of '1-4', where '1' is most important and '4' is least important. For example, a need requirement may be private medical insurance as most important to you, but because your company provides this and you have it, it will be a '4' on the scale. IHT reduction may be a '1' as important, and is an issue that must be resolved, as nothing has been done about yet.
5. Taking your circumstances into account (provided through a fact find usually), to produce a report leading to recommendations and an action plan.

The nil rate band

Every person or estate has a nil rate band of £325,000 in 2013/14 which rate is frozen to 2014/15 tax year. This is an estate exemption that means assets worth up to that amount will not be subject to inheritance tax. What many people do not know is that you can make use of the nil rate band whilst alive, and it is renewable every 7 years. You can therefore make your succession plan well in advance. Any gift you make to a person is out of your estate if you survive for at least 7 years. If you make a gift to a trust, then this is classed as a chargeable event and inheritance tax could be paid in advance at the rate of 20% of the value of the asset. However, the first £325,000, i.e. the nil rate band is exempt, so any gift made to the trust under this amount will be exempt. You can make the gift again in 7 years' time, when you get a new nil rate band! The growth in any investment made to the trust is also out of your estate.

Very wealthy people can make gifts to trust of amounts in excess of the nil rate band, or in addition to it, if the gift made is on a regular basis and made out of surplus regular income. This is another exemption from inheritance tax. If you assume someone has income of say £200,000 a year, and this is surplus to requirements, and can be paid to trust on a regular basis, then the gift out of normal expenditure rule (IHTA 1984 s.21) may apply to mitigate this income from inheritance tax.

A married couple or civil partners can make use of each other's nil rate bands for inheritance tax purposes. For example, if your spouse died before you and left all his assets to you, his nil rate band becomes transferable to your estate at the current rate. When you die, you have your nil rate band and the use of his unused portion of the nil rate band as well. In this tax year, £325,000 x 2 = £650,000 nil rate band exemptions. Proper planning is most important to ensure that you do get at least both nil rate bands. If one of the spouses has been married before, and her spouse has died, and she has remarried, she may even have three nil rate bands in her estate! Not bad planning, if you can get it.

Estate Planning includes dealing with bank accounts and the ownership of the house.

Bank accounts

Personal bank accounts could be 'frozen' on your death, and only available to your heirs after probate has been granted. This can cause financial problems on your death in respect of providing cash to the family or paying bills. A joint bank account overcomes this problem, if there is only one bank account available.

Ownership of the house

You can own the family home as either joint tenants or tenants in common or singly. If owned as a joint tenant (which is how the majority of property is held if married), on the death of one of the joint tenants, the share of the deceased automatically passes to the other joint tenant.

If the joint tenancy has been severed, then each owns his or her own share outright as a tenant in common. On death of a tenant in common, his or her share can pass by will or on intestacy. It does not pass automatically to the other partner or spouse.

It may be useful to sever the tenancy for a number of reasons. However, this can also cause problems. I recently had a client case where the client, a widow, wished to release equity from her home to provide for grandchildren's school fees. The only problem was that the house was half owned by her and half owned by a trust set up by her late husband. The equity release providers would not deal with the trust, and the property had to be transferred to the widow to deal with.

If the house is owned by one person, then the house can be left by will to anyone.

4

Long Term Care

As part of lifetime succession planning, there may be a possibility that you require long-term care, either at home, in hospital or in a specialist care home. Care fees are decided on an asset and income threshold test. The more you have, the more you pay, is the basic rule. Care fees in a private nursing home range from around £2,300 per month to £3,000 per month depending on location. These are funded by you, your relatives, and as a last resort, local councils/authorities. There are complex rules to prevent you from depriving your estate of assets (and if proved to be the case, these could be added back for the care fees calculation). However, certain assets, such as life assurance investment bonds are excluded property for the calculation. Forward planning is difficult, as you may not know if you will require care, unless it is immediate, or you have to plan around a family member who requires it.

Care fees plans are available, but few providers offer them.

	Lower	Upper
England	£14,250	£23,250
Wales	£23,750	£23,750
Scotland	£15,500	£25,250
Northern Ireland	£14,250	£23,250

If you have assets available valued at over £23,250 (England and Northern Ireland), £25,250 (Scotland), £23,750 (Wales) then you are liable for full care fees until your assets reduce to below various thresholds (England and Northern Ireland £14,250, Scotland £15,500, Wales £23,750). Your home is not included in the means test if a spouse, civil partner or partner resides in the property; any relative aged over 60 or is disabled resides in the property; a child under age 16 lives in the property; you are in the first 12 weeks of needing permanent care; or if the care is being provided on a temporary basis.

Couples are not assessed on their joint resources – only the person requiring care is assessed.

Funding for care may include available use of investments, income from pensions and state benefits, a care fees investment plan payable for life, and other methods, such as releasing equity from your home (used when you wish to be cared for in your own home).

You may need others to deal with your financial affairs, should you become mentally incompetent. Unless you have an old style EPA (Enduring power of attorney), from 1st October 2007 you require a Lasting Power of Attorney (LPA). Using an LPA, you plan ahead to the time when you may not have mental capacity and need to nominate others to take decisions on your behalf. If you do not have an LPA (Continuing Power of Attorney – CPA in Scotland), or an EPA, and you lose mental capacity, then a relative, friend or carer needs to apply to the Court of Protection to act as your agent – this is known as a 'Deputy'.

There are two types of LPA – one that deals with health and personal welfare, the other with financial affairs. The LPA must be registered with the Office of the Public Guardian before it can be used. The process of setting up an LPA can be expensive – but it is more convenient and ultimately less costly if you have to apply to the Court of Protection every time you wish to do something for the mentally incompetent person. LPA's, CPA's and EPA's continue if you become mentally incompetent, whereas an ordinary power of attorney ceases.

See *Long Term Care Simplified* by Tony Granger for more information.

$$5$$

Retirement Planning

Retirement planning is not just about personal and occupational pension schemes, and the State pension. It is also about the accumulation of savings and investments, and takes into account property, such as the family home, which can be downsized or used to generate capital and income, through equity release. There may also be business and employment issues to be considered.

Succession planning in the retirement planning sense is concerned with the following:

* Providing for dependants if death occurs before retirement
* Providing for dependants if death occurs after retirement
* Possibly providing for inheritance taxes caused by pension scheme funds going to the estate
* Ill-health before and after retirement

Death before retirement

Depending on where you are in the life cycle, will determine your overall dependants' needs, as well as what will be available to them.

If death occurs at an early stage in your career, then it is likely that not a great deal of pension funding will have been accumulated. Later on, one would expect larger pension and savings funds to have been accumulated.

If you die 'in service' then the pension fund rules will usually stipulate what sort of death benefits are payable.

Employers' pension schemes may have death in service benefits, arising from the pension fund itself, or provided through group scheme life assurance. The latter is usually provided up to retirement age and then ceases.

Group life cover (death in service benefits) is defined as a multiple of salary, for example, two or four times your final remuneration, or as a fixed benefit. It is payable to named beneficiaries or dependants. Payments made by the life cover trustees, for tax reasons, are always discretionary, but they do usually follow a letter of wishes left with them.

If there are no death in service insured benefits then with private pension schemes, such as personal pension schemes, SIPPs and most money purchase defined contribution pension schemes will usually return the value of the pension fund to date. However some schemes will only return your own contributions plus a growth factor, such as 4%. The latter is the worst deal, especially if single premium contributions have been made. Some product providers may change the basis to a return of fund if asked. Check the policy wording carefully.

Payments made on death before retirement are usually tax free. These funds can be used to purchase a widow's/widower's pension and dependants' pensions. Dependants' pensions provided on death before retirement do not count towards the standard lifetime allowance. There is technically no limit on benefits that can be provided for dependants on death before retirement. A spouse or civil partner and children (usually two) age under age 23 (later ages may be acceptable under exceptional circumstances) will automatically qualify. If an unmarried couple, then you must show financial dependency to receive a dependant's pension.

A return of fund and pension contributions paid as well as death in service life assurance can be paid tax free, so long as the payments overall are within the standard lifetime allowance, which is £1.5 million from 2013/14. Lump sums paid in excess of the standard lifetime allowance will be subject to tax at 55% (unless funds are protected).

If you have insufficient pension funding or death in service benefits, then you may need to self –insure in order to provide tax free death benefits yourself. Lump sums provided in this way can be invested to provide for more tax efficient pension or annuity income.

Death after retirement

Once you have retired from your pension fund, you will be receiving your monthly pension or annuity, or drawdown income.

The type of death benefits available will depend on the type of scheme you are in and whether there are any guarantees to continue with dependants' pensions or not.

Occupational pension scheme

If an occupational pension scheme, and you are single, pension benefits will cease. If there are guarantees attaching to your fund to pay out for a minimum period, then such payments will be paid to your estate or nominated beneficiary. If married, your spouse or civil partner will receive usually a reduced pension, but this depends on the scheme rules. The range is in the area of 50% to 66% of your pension. These pension schemes are valuable as they usually have increasing pensions, RPI linked.

Money purchase pension scheme

If your funding was through a personal pension fund or money purchase arrangements, you would be either in drawdown (drawing down an income from the scheme) or you will have taken out an annuity, or have a scheme pension paid from your funds. An annuity could be with or without guarantees, and for a single life or on a joint life basis. if a single life annuity, on your death, the annuity ceases.(unless there is a guarantee to pay the annuity for a certain period which it will do). If a joint and survivor annuity, then on the first death, the annuity continues to pay to the survivor for their lifetime – often at a reduced rate. If there is a term certain guarantee, then notwithstanding both deaths, the annuity will continue to pay until the end of the guarantee period – often to the estate or possibly to dependants. It is possible to insure your fund and to take a single life annuity which will give you a higher income. On your death the annuity ceases, but the life assurance pays out tax free to provide an income for dependants.

Drawdown schemes

If your fund is in 'drawdown' you have not decided to take an annuity or scheme pension, and are drawing down pension income according to the government actuary's GAD limits. There are three options for a surviving spouse or civil partner under drawdown.

1. A return of fund less 55% tax charge – you have two years to take up this option, or
2. The remaining fund buys a single annuity (note the requirement to take an annuity is abolished from 6.4.2011), or
3. To continue with drawdown, after paying a tax charge. Dependant children under age 18 can also benefit – up to age 23 if in full time education.

There are new income drawdown rules that apply from 2011/12, and the old categories of USP (up to age 77) and ASP (after age 77) have been abolished, to be replaced with capped and flexible drawdown. If you die during drawdown, your spouse can continue with drawdown or take an annuity, or have a lump sum payment.

If you die before age 75, the remaining funds can be paid as a cash lump sum, subject to a tax charge of 55% from 6.4.2011 if you have not taken benefits yet, and if over age 75, whether or not you have taken benefits, the tax charge is also 55%. Whilst lower than the previous tax charge of 82%, this is still a significant tax charge.

It is unlikely that any death in service benefits or group scheme benefits will be available to be paid after retirement, unless you have funded personally for this event.

In almost all instances it would be wise to arrange to have lump sum death benefits to be paid in trust outside of the estate. This avoids probate and inheritance tax and the proceeds can be paid direct to the beneficiaries.

Inheritance tax on pension funds

Note that after the second death (spouse or civil partner) – or first death if no dependants, the balance of any pension fund remaining is payable to the estate and may be liable for taxes – up to 55%. This can be avoided by payments to charity of the fund residue. The pension fund residue payable to the estate is reduced by any available nil rate band amount.

Ill health and early retirement

Most occupational pension funds allow you to retire early for reasons of ill-health. You retire on a reduced amount, in terms of the scheme rules. The rules on death before and after retirement will apply as above.

Investments and savings

Depending on your personal circumstances, your investments and savings will be used to provide for income in retirement. Until then, they will usually be growth investments. If you have a dutiable estate that may suffer inheritance tax, you should consider 'wrapping' your investments, or making them in trust, to avoid such taxes (at 40%). Investments such as ISAs, bonds, shares, property etc., fall into your estate for inheritance tax purposes. An inheritance tax wrapper for an investment bond could result in a discounted gift trust (DGT), for example. With a DGT investment bond an amount would be immediately out of your estate for IHT purposes, the balance falling out after 7 years. An EIS investment if held for 2 years will be fully out of your estate. Whilst generally higher risk, you can now have capital protected EIS investments.

It is essential that investment planning also includes tax planning. Personal capital gains tax exemptions are £10,900 each in the 2013/14 tax year, which means you can take income as growth from your investments and not pay any tax on the first £10,900 worth of capital gains.

Your house

The family home is an important consideration for retirement as well as post death planning. If there is a mortgage, then this needs to be repaid or reduced in the event of death. At retirement you may wish to trade down or move to another area, or even retire abroad.

The house can also be a store of value. Equity release arrangements enable you to draw down capital from your house that can be invested. The interest payable rolls up against the value of the house. The house is sold on the death of the last dying (or if the last survivor moves into long term care), and the equity release provider recoups its investment at this time.

You also need to decide how to decide on what to do with the house as far as your wills are concerned, and whether to hold it as single tenants in common or as joint tenants.

6

Health, Disability and income protection

If you suffer ill health or disability, or a dread disease or critical illness, then you may not be able to work and earn a living. This will severely affect your ongoing succession planning. A fundamental and core protection is to protect the family's income going forward.

A number of income protection plans are available should you become seriously ill and cannot work. Some employers will pay 6 months' salary, others less. After that, you're on your own (unless you have income protection as an employee benefit) and have to make your own arrangements. The Government incapacity benefit is now called the Employment and Support Allowance (ESA). This is paid after statutory sick pay comes to an end. The weekly rate range is from £71.70 per week (£286.80 per month) at the lower limit, and up to £101.35 per week (£405.40 month) at the higher rate. (Short term incapacity benefit if under state pension age).

Income protection (PHI) policies will pay a benefit through to retirement age, usually between 50-60% of your salary.

Critical illness (CIC) policies pay out a lump sum on diagnosis of a dread disease, or critical illness, such as cancer, stroke, paraplegia, heart attack. You may suffer a dread disease (the CIC policy pays out), but can still work, so the PHI policy may not pay out, until you cannot work, when it will do so.

In August 2012 a total of 2,6 million people were on incapacity benefit in UK, amounting to 7% of the population of working age. (DWP statistics).

Protecting your future succession plans are a key component of your overall planning.

7

Succession Planning and Divorce

Your circumstances will dictate your financial planning. You may be divorced and may have remained single, or remarried. Children from a previous marriage may be added to children from a new marriage; or new children from a new spouse may be introduced into the family. All of these aspects require consideration and planning.

Your divorce order will determine your range of planning. For example, you may have had to split your pension funds with your former spouse on divorce. This will mean that you will have less funds to consider in retirement if the payer; and more funds to consider in retirement if the recipient.

Over the last 15 years the rate of divorce has been gradually declining in the UK, but 2011 saw a small rise, up 4.9% from the previous year to 119,589 divorces in England and Wales. One in five men and women divorcing in 2011 had a previous marriage ending in divorce. This proportion has doubled in 32 years: in 1980 one in ten men and women divorcing had a previous marriage ending in divorce. Sixty-nine per cent of divorces were by couples where the marriage was the first for both parties.

As far as wills are concerned, divorce does not automatically revoke your old will. However:-

- If a couple divorces, but one or both spouses have not changed their wills and one spouse dies, or if one spouse dies before a divorce is final? If a spouse dies while a divorce or dissolution of marriage is in process, but not yet final, the other spouse will inherit under the will. Once the divorce is final, gifts to an ex-spouse in a will are no longer valid unless the will specifically says the gifts should be valid, even in the event of divorce. An ex-spouse can inherit, but the intent to provide for the ex-spouse must be clearly stated in the will.
- A divorce treats former spouses as if they were omitted from the Will. No gift will pass to them, and even if they are named as executors they cannot act as such. However, the rest of the Will remains valid.

You must decide whether you want an ex spouse to inherit under your will. If not, review your will after their divorce. Even if you do wish to include an ex spouse, then review your will as the ex spouse is exactly that – not 'I leave everything to my wife'.

If either spouse already has a will which named the former spouse as a beneficiary that provision will be automatically revoked by decree absolute. It is better to write a completely new will after a divorce.

Civil partnerships

The dissolution of a civil partnership has the same effect on the partners' Wills as does divorce for married couples. The formation of a civil partnership revokes the partner's Will unless made in contemplation of their civil partnership.

Ongoing commitments

If there has been a clean break divorce there is no need for a new will to make any provision for the former spouse. However, sometimes one spouse pays the former spouse maintenance or periodical payments following the divorce. In that case the former spouse is still a 'dependant' and so a new will needs to take that account.

An important area for consideration here is that where there is a court order where you have ongoing maintenance commitments for former spouse and children, and you die, these commitments do not necessarily die with you. Being of a contractual nature, your estate could be liable for ongoing maintenance payments until the happening of the event that terminates it – for example until the former spouse remarries or dies. Your planning will be to provide for this in your estate – your former spouse could be 'inheriting' before your new spouse.

Note the rule about invalidating gifts to ex-spouses in your will doesn't apply to trusts, insurance policies, retirement plans, or instruments like living wills. All of these must be changed to exclude the ex-spouse if that's desired. Because many people use living trusts (set up whilst you are alive, as opposed to coming into effect on your death) instead of wills to transfer the bulk of their property at death to avoid the delays and costs of probate, it's very important to remember to change living trusts after a divorce.

The house

Where there is a female (usually) ex- spouse with children, it is usual that the male needs to find another house. Whilst both parties will be involved in their own succession planning, the planning base of the 'paying' party will have been severely eroded.

Remarriage

If you get remarried or married, this usually revokes or cancels a previous will.

As a result you could find you have no Will at all and the intestacy rules would apply.

Separation

If you are separated and live apart, you will still be married in the eyes of the law. Unless you change your wills and beneficiary nominations on life policies, pension plans and trusts, your spouse will still benefit from you (if this is what you want).

Co-habitees

Succession planning for divorcing couples is important. However, considerably more people simply live together, have children and do not get married.

Planning here is absolutely vital, as on death or separation, there could only be a claim for dependency.

If there is no will, and a partner dies intestate, the other partner is not 'family' and will not inherit. He or she may not benefit from a partner's pension funds, life policies or other assets.

Key points summary

Succession planning for individuals takes into account your total assets and liabilities and your objectives and goals for the future. Various life planning events have been considered, including death, retirement, disability and the inability to work, family events such as divorce and separation, and the effect of taxes and how to avoid them. The individual needs to develop check lists and aims and objectives. These will include who is to benefit from death and on retirement, and by how much.

Part 2

Business Succession Planning

Succession planning for businesses applies to business owners as well as to the people in the business. The traditional concept of succession planning includes finding a replacement for a key person, in the event of death, disability, retirement, or career advancement. It is the identification of future potential leaders within the organisation, as well as externally, and the planned career path of such leaders for the future success of the business. Identified successors could be short-term, or those with longer-term potential.

Succession planning is about determining the future and the anticipation of likely changes, and how best to map out a route to accomplish your objectives and scenario plans. In the final analysis, it may involve a transfer of power as well as control of the business. The reason why succession planning takes place well in advance of the proposed event is to ensure as smooth a transition as possible, and with the greatest effectiveness. There is no one success model and no hard and fast rules. What works for one organisation or business, may be an abject failure for another.

The succession plan should be documented. It could involve the identification of key people to manage an organisation; it will, for the owner-manager or business owners be integral to retirement planning or selling the business because the time is right for this. The preservation of wealth on the one hand (not making a hasty sale or business exit), and the continuation of the business without the business owner being there (often to ensure an ongoing payout programme) will be key determinants.

Obtaining a successful result is the most important aspect. Business wealth creation involves a large amount of risk taking. The value of the business will be represented by its profits and assets, and the value of its shares or partnership value. If the business sale or exit is largely unplanned, much of the value could be lost in taxation, the loss of a key person with valuable business contacts; and no continuity planning.

For the multi-owner business, the planning process may not be as difficult when compared with the family company, or partnerships, which may require a different kind of planning. The sole trader business may be valuable to the sole trader, but without him, there may be no business. Succession planning therefore will involve business advisers and tax planners working closely with business owners. For the larger business, possibly listed on the stock exchange, the planning scenarios will be completely different. Smaller businesses often have as their main objectives cash flow and survival and the risks for the business owner personally will be greater than the CEO of a PLC who is looking for a business exit through flotation or merger where share price and profits are the major determinants. Individually though, that same CEO will be looking to maximise his returns and personal wealth in the same way that the business owner will be creating wealth to exit the business at a later.

Features for Business Succession Planning

8

Creating the Succession Plan

The first step in business succession planning is to create the succession plan. This involves stating your personal and business objectives and then developing strategies for each objective. Over the course of time, business and personal objectives will change, as your circumstances change. Internal and external factors will come into play, and must be taken into account. For example, you may decide to exit the business in two years' time, by way of a trade sale. Unfortunately the global credit crunch comes along, and the supply of funds to purchase your business share has dried up. This is an external factor that could delay your business exit.

The following are key factors that should be in any succession plan.

Set your objectives

Personal and Business objectives, aims and desires for the business owners are usually inter-linked. The business pays salaries and dividends or bonuses, and provides benefits. The better the business can do, the better the individual is able to benefit from wealth creation.

Also bear in mind that it is not only the business owners who see the business as the wealth pool. Employees and dependants are also totally reliant on the business for their wealth creation.

List Your Personal Objectives

Some examples are:
- Use the business to create wealth for the business owners
- Retire successfully at age 60
- Pensions and savings plans for retirement
- Ensure family and business protection is in place
- Investments to be efficient
- To fund the children's education
- Pay off the mortgage as early as possible
- Tax planning to be efficient now and at the point of sale
- Provide adequately for spouse and dependants
- Make sure wills are up to date and valid
- Make sure trusts are valid and effective

- Make sure income protection is in place
- Make sure disability and health plans are adequate
- Personal lifestyle planning fulfilment and needs
- To have a track to run on and a monitoring process
- To have a personal financial plan

List Your Business Objectives

Some examples are:
- To have an up to date business plan, showing the figures.
- Investigate areas to cut costs and to make savings
- Identify key people in the business
- Identify likely successors
- Training and grooming of likely successors
- Ensure business agreements are valid and in place
- Ensure shareholder agreements are valid and in place (or partnership agreements)
- Decide on a strategy for employee motivation
- Decide on a strategy for employee benefits
- Objectives for retirement from the business
- To exit the business in the best possible way
- To utilise tax reliefs and plan for entrepreneur's relief
- To research ways to fund the exit
- To have business protection strategies for keypeople
- To have business risk management strategies in place to protect the business
- To create business wealth. To add value to the business
- To preserve and increase business wealth
- To ensure that employees and management are taken care of when the business is sold
- To ensure that all business advisers are aware of their planning inputs
- To communicate what must be communicated to employees and stakeholders

Once individual personal and business objectives are known, a matrix can be built of common objectives amongst the business owners. This will assist the business owners to strive to achieve the highest level of satisfaction of common objectives for all concerned. That is not to say that certain personal and business objectives will be ignored because they are not common to all parties, but it is an opportunity to attend not only to the greater good, but also to accommodate individual personal or business needs requirements.

For example, after assessing personal and business objectives, the following matrix results:

Common Personal Objectives
Tax Efficiency
* To use the business to create personal wealth
* Business owners to exit/retire/sell their share on average by age 60
* Business owners want cash for their shares
* Business owners want maximum pension funding
* Business owners have a need to fund for school or university fees
* Business owners wish to maximise employee benefits to save on personal costs

Common Business Objectives
* To have a defined succession plan to exit the business
* To insure the business owners to enable cash to be paid for their shares on death
* To fund a business pension plan at maximum levels
* To have employee and director/partner group schemes and employee benefits
* To have an education trust funded by the business for children and dependants
* To employ tax-efficient arrangements now and in the future
* To identify successors and to train them or recruit externally
* To focus on wealth creation and building business value
* To create profits and minimise losses and costs

This can best be described as the 'thinking stage'. It provides a core focus area for the business owners on what they wish the business to achieve. These objectives can then be translated into goals. Goals should be defined and given time lines and implemented if accepted. Along with objectives and goals is commitment. Commitment is best described in writing. Write down your goals and objectives and give a reasonable time period to achieve these.

9

Create a Business Plan

This is no bad thing in any event. Often a business plan is required to support bank funding or financing, or is required for share valuations. Knowing the figures is all important. Many business owners are content to let the finance director or accountant run the show, and to be aware of the business data and figures and other financials. However, these financials can be largely historical and for many is not entirely accurate. The business owner may have a particular expertise, such as marketing or client acquisition and does not have time to pore over the books. Make time. This is essential. Too many businesses fail because the hand guiding the rudder does not take care of the essentials. You, as a business owner, are also vulnerable through lack of financial knowledge, which can be exploited by others.

I have seen this in a slightly different context. Ask any business owner where the biggest costs in the business are, after pay and payroll. Most will say IT. The problem is the vast majority of people do not know what that IT person or team does, and usually accepts the position. Upgrading IT in a business to increase capacity can also involve the cost of new hardware, internet servers and the like, when possibly the existing equipment can actually do the job.

Business plan components

- Have an upfront summary of where the business is now and where it wishes to be in 1 year through to 3 or 5 years.
- Some say that to have a 'mission statement' is passé and past its sell by date. However, stating the main business objectives and how they are to be achieved can create a focus point for all the people in the business.
- Structure of the business. Who the business owners are and in what proportions do they share in the business.
- If a company, shares in issue, share valuations. Identify share owners, their percentages and their ages. Ages are important as some may be closer to retirement and business exits than others.
- If a partnership or LLP (Limited Liability Partnership), the partners and their shares; their capital and current accounts; their ages.
- Balance sheet noting the assets and liabilities of the business
- Profit and loss statement

- Cash flows now and expected in the future
- Marketing, Sales and Distribution – targets and performance
- Diagrammatic chart of personnel and key positions
- Business financial requirements for working capital and expenditure

are some of the key components. Others can be added as they are identified.

You can construct the business plan yourself or bring in professional planners to help you. Your accountant can assist with draft accounts (or actual) and you can add the other components that you deem essential.

You must decide which areas can be handled by you, as business owner, and which areas will require outside help and expertise. There is an old adage that the entrepreneurial business owner begins planning his or her business exit on the day the business is first set up. The thought processes will always be how to make the business better, more successful, more profitable. Where can value be added and how; where is cash haemorrhaging from the business and why; what do you need in the business and what can you do without? Challenge everything, accept nothing at face value.

The business plan forms the basis of your succession plan.

10

Identify Possible Exit Routes

It is important to think about exit routes at an early stage. The type of exit route selected will also point you in the direction of how to develop the business for the best possible exit in financial terms. The business could be sold as a whole, with all stakeholders making money from it. Alternatively, there may be a piecemeal exit of business owners as they reach retirement age, and want value for their shareholdings. On the one hand, if all business owners exit at the same time, then new business owners step in and take over the business. If the exit planned is for retirement, death or incapacity affecting a single business owner at any one time, then the survivors remain to carry on the business, possibly without a fee earner, or sales generator, or manager, who will have to be replaced. The thinking will be different for each scenario.

We then also have situations where some kinds of business exit will be effective and others not. For example, take the family owned company. Traditionally, shares are held by the family and are not offered to employees; only other family members are accepted into the ownership hierarchy; some may wish to sell and others not. How does the family business owner who wishes to retire, and has a minority (or majority) of the shares accomplish this? Similarly, professional partnerships (accountants, solicitors, doctors, architects etc.) or LLPs, will need to plan individual exits well in advance – in this case, it is unlikely that a whole practice will be sold, but if it is, then the sales route needs to be identified.

Whilst covered later in wealth creation strategies, the mindset of different businesses' owners will vary depending on the type of exit route selected and the type of business you are in.

For example, if a business made up of non-family non-dependant shareholders, their aim will be to increase profits annually, to not spend or distribute profits unless absolutely necessary, to reduce costs wherever possible and to show year on year growth. This should give them an increasing share price and the best possible share value at exit.

Compare this to a family company of inter-dependant members and shareholders, who are not preparing to exit the business at any time. They can take out what they want, when they want, and have a far more relaxed approach to business. As long as the business is profitable and sustainable, these business owners may not necessarily be that phased if value is added to the business, and are more content to build their value outside the business, by taking profits out of it. The more saleable business will be the one that shows increasing profitability and growth on a year on year basis.

A partnership or LLP member could be typical of extreme personal wealth maximisation. Each individual is building his share not necessarily for the whole business, but for himself. This is reflected in individual capital and current accounts. For many partnerships, their clients and fee earning capability belong to them (personal fiefdoms spring to mind), and they are generally intent on building personal wealth. Yes, they will contribute to the greater good, but personal responsibility on business cash flowing is very much theirs. This approach also inhibits joint decision-making, which can sometimes be tortuous. This type of partner is also very much aware of what his partnership or LLP agreement will state on him exiting the business. I have seen solicitors' partnership and LLP agreements where a retiring partner's capital account (his share of value in the business) is repaid to him monthly over a ten year period. (His capital in the business is still required for working capital). He has left the business and is totally dependent on the survivors in the business continuing making payments to him. The partnership mindset must change to building better business value and ensuring a fair exit for individuals within reasonable time frames for all.

Exit routes where the company as a whole is sold

The most common forms of exit routes where the business as a whole is sold and the business owners maximise their return from the business sale are as follows:

*   **Trade sale** – the business is sold to a competitor or new entrant. The sale is usually for cash and or loan notes; often for a mix of shares in the new business entity and cash and loan notes. It may be purchased by individuals who raise capital, or have the use of private equity funding groups using venture capital to do so.

*   **Management Buy-out or Management Buy-in**. A management team raises the cash to buy out the business owners. This usually involves debt raised against the assets of the business. Often the business itself becomes so burdened with debt, it fails. For bigger businesses, expect a venture capital company to back the sale and purchase. This involves taking a stake in the business. If a smaller business, the management team raise personal finance through remortgaging their houses or taking personal loans to purchase the business.

*   **Using Employees**. Your employees could be more valuable than you think. Firstly, they can create a market for your shares, where one would

not normally exist. Employees can build up capital to buy shares through SAYE plans, and then purchase shares. An employee share owner trust or QUEST (qualifying employee share trust) can be set up by the company. The company can fund the trust and the funds provided can be used to purchase shares from shareholders for the use of employees. These types of share trusts are very popular and allowable by HMRC. The contributions made by the company to the share trust can be deductible from taxable profits. A common funding method is to fund a pension scheme (SIPPs/ SSAS) that allow loans at 50% of the scheme assets to be made to the company. The pension contributions are deductible to the company. The payment to the share trust is also allowable. This could be a most effective and tax efficient planning for an exit route. If a single shareholder, the trust could arrange for life assurance on the shareholder to buy his shares if he dies, thus ensuring cash is paid to his estate.

- **Listing the Shares**. If the company qualifies through size and cash resources (for fees) to obtain a stock market listing, this is an exit route for successful growth companies. Initial capital could be raised on AIM (Alternative Investment Market) for quoted shares or the Plus market, where unquoted company shares can be traded. Some companies can graduate to the main stock market from AIM, once they have established a track record and can afford the fees for a full listing.

Exit routes – where a partial sale of shares is made

- **Other shareholders.** Remaining shareholders can buy the shares of the exiting shareholder(s). In fact, some companies' articles and memoranda do not allow the sale of shares to outsiders, before first being offered to existing shareholders. This route depends on the desirability of buying more shares, and at what price. (CA 1985, s 162(2); CA 2006, s 692(2)). Individuals use existing funds or take loans or remortgages to make the share purchase. This could also be the position where a new shareholder wishes to purchase shares from existing shareholders.

- **Management and Employees.** As above for the full sale of the business.

- **Company buys back its own shares.** This is a route to consider. The company buys back shares and cancels them. Any payment in excess of the original capital subscribed for the shares will be a distribution and treated as income. (ICTA 1988 s 209(2)(b). But for unquoted trading companies, there is an exception if conditions are satisfied, and the seller is treated as receiving a capital distribution. This could be a tax efficient exit route. Shares must be purchased out of distributable profits or the proceeds of a new share issue to finance the purchase (CA 1985, s

162(2); CA 2006, s 692(2)).. Shares could be purchased out of capital if an unquoted company. (CA 1985, ss 160(1), 171-177; CA 2006, ss 692(1), 709-723).

- **Venture Capital**. A venture capital company could stake- build through individual share purchase.

- **Other Companies**. Similarly, companies or other business entities could purchase the shares. Note, however, under the corporate venturing rules, an outgoing shareholder could not sell his or her shares to another company wishing to obtain tax relief on the purchase under the previous corporate venturing rules. This is because the shares to be sold must be newly issued shares, and only the company selling shares can do this.

Non- company exit routes

These would apply to sole traders and partnerships in the main.

What must be determined is what exactly is being sold, or offered for sale. If it was a company then shares in the company would be sold. If a sole trader, there are no company shares, and the sale price could include assets and goodwill. If a partnership, it would be the partnership share, which could include the capital and current accounts, as well as goodwill and assets.

Professional partnerships and LLPs, such as solicitors and accountants, doctors, dentists would require the proposed sale to an incoming partner to be a qualified individual (i.e. another solicitor, accountant etc.). However, one can now be a partner of many different types of professional practice, without being qualified as such, as their practice rules can allow for this.

Setting a time line

Once the possible exit strategy has been determined, set a time line for the exit. It may be more immediate – within the next 2-3 years, or longer-term, say in 7- 10 years time.

Example

The business **value** now is £2 million. The ambitious entrepreneur wishes to grow the business and double the value every two years:

Year 1:	£2,000,000
Year 3:	£4,000,000
Year 5:	£8,000,000
Year 7:	£16,000,000
Year 10:	£32,000,000

He sets the time line to exit the business in 5 years' time for a business value of £8 million.

He can now work backwards and build his growth plan accordingly – knowing what the end result will be. What does he need to do to accomplish this objective? It may be that, after working out a unit cost of profitability, with a larger business model, he can achieve greater economies of scale, and the costs per unit of profitability will come down (thus increasing profits). Alternatively, initial costs could be higher as he needs to tool up and/or 'staff up 'the organisation to have the means of production and people to achieve his objectives. He could also make acquisitions of other businesses to increase profitability faster.

The identified exit route from his initial thoughts (at this stage, circumstances may change in the future and different exits need to be continually re-assessed) are to (i) build a management team who will buy the business or (ii) identify potential purchasers for a trade sale.

Working on the business (as opposed to merely in it) means that the budding entrepreneur needs to plan ahead, not only with a phased business growth model, but also to identify successors and a strong management team to take the business forward. The business plan is the starting point. Scenario planning follows from that.

11

Valuing the Business

A business is seen as an investment medium and its value is determined by the future returns it offers. Identifying the factors that provide an opportunity to maximise these returns from the business provides a solid base for both setting a valuation and developing future plans to enhance business performance.

Existing and potential business owners who appreciate current business investment values can make informed decisions and maximize opportunities when they arise.

The two questions 'How much is your business worth?' and 'How can you make it more valuable?' are of paramount importance to any business owner.

The worth of a business hinges upon how much profit a purchaser can make from it, balanced by the risks involved. Past profitability and asset values are only the starting points. It is often intangible factors, such as key business relationships, which provide the most value.

There are literally thousands of permutations on how to value the business. The true value of a business is what someone might pay for it. On the other hand, unless a **valuation formula** is agreed upfront between purchaser and seller, there may not be agreement on price and responsibility going forward. The sale will just not go through. For example, it may be a condition of sale that the seller, once the sale is made, remains with the business to ensure its smooth transition for say two years. He may not wish to do this. Part of the sale deal may be an 'earn-out' to accomplish the sale price. This means there is no immediate exit from the business. From the buyer's point of view, especially with a service or customer based sales business, to retain the seller for a period of time makes sense, as customers could be lost immediately with a new owner.

The sales agreement would also include important legal clauses to protect the purchaser and their future viability and profitability. These would include covenants on not starting up in competition with the business taken over for a certain period of time, and may be geographically restrictive as well. It may also involve tying in certain key people for a period of time to ensure continuity of the business.

You must also agree on exactly what is being bought and what is being sold. You may only be selling shares in a company. However, you own the property premises, from where the company trades, or the premises are owned by your pension scheme, and you do not wish to sell the property as well. However, the purchaser is under the impression that the premises are part of the deal. You need to stipulate exactly what is being purchased and sold to avoid any misunderstanding later.

Effective **due diligence** is key to any sale. That means going over every contract, lease agreement, marketing agreement, employment contracts, customer data base and other important areas to ensure that you buy exactly what is being sold. Some years ago a major UK accountancy firm raised capital for an expanding business which manufactured plastic garden plant trays for the horticultural trade. This business was booming, and required expansion capital to purchase new machinery for production and to expand into valuable European markets. Just the thing for private investors, and they invested in their droves. However, shortly after the finance was raised, a bid to purchase the company was made by the main and only (exclusive) distributor of the products, which was turned down. The distributor responded by saying they would not distribute any of the products unless the company was sold to them, and because they held an exclusive distribution agreement, the company manufacturer could not turn to anyone else to distribute their products. In the end the company collapsed and investors lost their money. Due diligence should have discovered this exclusive marketing agreement and either a new deal done, or the current expansion deal avoided. The question is how far do you go in making due diligence enquiries? The answer is as far as possible.

By not taking these precautions, not only might you, the purchaser have unpleasant surprises down the line, but that these could reduce the value of the sale.

For the seller, the above points are things to be prepared for. The astute purchaser will want to see your books of account, as well as contracts and other paperwork that may affect the outcome of the sale and its price. By acting ahead of the curve, you can influence the pricing significantly, and achieve an optimum result.

How, then should the business be valued? The seller wants the best price, as does the buyer. More often than not, these pricing values do not exactly meet, and need to be negotiated. As stated before, the first point of agreement is what exactly is for sale? Then agree on a valuation formula. Then agree on what the terms of the buy-and-sell will be.

The main valuation methods are as follows:

Net asset value method

This is one of the least controversial methods. Assets less liabilities give you a value. This is also known as the 'adjusted book value'. Linked to this is asset valuation, often used where businesses carry physical assets in inventory.

This method is often used for businesses that are losing money. The value of the business is based essentially on what the current assets of the business are worth.

There may be Specific Intangible Assets, where for example, a customer base would be valuable to a purchaser. The value of the business is based on how much it would have cost the buyer to generate this intangible asset themselves.

Asset valuations are appropriate, for example, where tangible assets, such as a property business, is being sold.

Rate of return method/cash flows

A common starting point is to use a price/earnings ratio, if the business is making substantial profits.

The discounted cash flow method is a calculation is based on future cash flow. It is appropriate for businesses which have invested heavily and are forecasting steady cash flow over many years.

Profitable businesses may wish the dividend yield method to be used. This may include the dividend yield of the business, where a value is placed on the business share dependant on its profitability and its ability to pay dividends.

Often income and earnings are capitalised. A valuation where *income* is capitalised is frequently used by service organizations because it places the greatest value on intangibles while giving no credit for physical assets. Capitalisation is defined as the return on investment that is expected. Business strengths are rated to obtain a capitalisation rate which is used as multiplication factor of the discretionary income to arrive at the business' value.

Earnings of the business can be capitalised, based on the rate of return in earnings that the investor expects. For no risk investments, an investor would expect eight percent. Small businesses usually are expected to have a rate of return of 25 percent. Consequently, if your business has expected earnings of £75,000, its value might be estimated at £300,000 (300,000 x 25% = £75,000).

An 'excess earnings' method is used where the return on assets is separated from other earnings which are interpreted as the "excess" earnings you generate. Usually return on assets is estimated from an industry average.

One of the most common methods used for valuing a business is a multiple of earnings. In this method a multiple of the cash flow of the business is used to calculate its value.

Other valuers may use discounted cash flows which are based on the assumption that a pound received today is worth more than one received in the future. It discounts the business's projected earnings to adjust for real growth, inflation and risk.

A valuation method often used by managers to buy out the business MBO/MBI) is the debt assumption method which usually gives the highest price. It is based on how much debt a business could have and still operate, using cash flow to pay the debt.

Intrinsic value method

This is a hybrid of valuations, which may include net assets, plus the value of income streams, future spend values of clients of the business, and other factors such as cash flows and income streams.

A multiplier or market valuation which uses an industry average sales figure from recent business sales in comparable businesses as a multiplier can be used. For example, the industry multiplier for a marketing company might be .75 which is multiplied by annual gross sales to arrive at the value of the business.

The entry cost method values a business by reference to the cost of starting up a similar business from scratch.

Industry 'rules of thumb' is one method to determine an established, standard formula for the particular sector for business valuation.

Super-profits method

Any of the other methods used, plus goodwill.

Why you need a valuation?

You will need a valuation for your succession plan to determine business value now and in the future. Think about the different valuation methods, and which would be most appropriate for you, considering profitability, cash flows now and in the future, earnings now and in the future, cost reduction, what the sector pricing model is, and what you are prepared to sell the business for. Bear in mind the other side of the fence – what does the purchaser wish to purchase and why? What is he buying? Is it only assets, or the business itself, including many more things with an intrinsic value, such as the customer base and intellectual property? What is not included in the sale?

12

Negotiating the Best Price

The seller will have a price in mind, the buyer a different price. These pricing mechanisms could be miles apart. The purchaser may only see net asset values, whilst the seller sees the goodwill of the customer base, as well as future flows in the valuation. Even though it may seem unreasonable to the seller – as more often than not, there is some emotion connected with selling a business you have built up over many years; to the buyer, it is a cold, calculated purchase and the best price is to be obtained for it.

Often skilled negotiators need to negotiate the best price for the seller. On average, the buyer can be pushed to up to 30% more if the business is properly prepared for sale.

There can be many obstacles in the buy/sell process. For example, a business may be a fantastic proposition, but may have pension funding liabilities, that the new purchaser does not wish to assume – result equals no sale.

How to calculate profits for valuation purposes

The potential purchaser will wish to ascertain what the true profitability is when considering making a purchase of the business.

The first step is to examine the current books of account and financials and to compare the owner's stated profits with the audited figures. Any differences should be questioned.

The next step is to see where you would reduce costs. These would include cheaper suppliers, payments to the shareholders or owners and others, including redundancy payments, reducing pension overheads and employee costs (the most expensive part of any business, other than IT). Consultancy fees, unnecessary leases and properties (where activities could be combined or rationalised), duplicate overheads are all areas to consider. For example, one business allowed each executive to subscribe to publications at a cost of £110,000 per annum. This was reduced to £2,500 with readership being circulated.

It is important to use your own accounting policies when calculating the business profits. Some costs may have been capitalised by the present owner, whereas they could have been restated as costs (for example, software).

There may be costs involved in achieving future profits.

More often than not, if increased borrowings are involved, the cost of servicing these borrowings may increase. Likewise, the existing business owner may have given personal guarantees to the bank for bank finance and you may not be prepared to do so. Servicing increased borrowings can be costly. There may be staffing costs involved with redundancy payments or new hires, pension scheme payments where pension schemes have been underfunded in the past, or even tax liabilities that have yet to be met. There is also the depreciation of investment in plant, machinery, or new technology.

The arrival of new management often leads to major changes which may mean higher costs and lower productivity in the first year.

Increasing business value

Adding value to the business enables you to increase the price at which you sell it. Increasing business value is usually measured through increased profits or return on investment.

Inherent in the business value equation is reducing costs and taxation. Profits made can actually stay the same, so long as costs are reduced, as well as taxation, to increase value.

Some years ago I developed a business valuation formula, to show how business consultants can add value.

The business value formula

What is the overriding, decisive objective of the majority of business owners?

$$\Sigma \, (IP + RP) \times [M] = AV + IAV$$

Where:

Σ	=	the sum of
IP	=	Improved Profit
RP	=	Risk Protection
M	=	free Cashflow multiplier
AV	=	Added value
IAV	=	Intrinsic Added Value

Improved profit is the result of cost reduction and tax reduction, which is immediately added to the bottom line. Cost reduction could be attained through various cost-reduction audits and strategies. These may be a corporate benefit audit, where for example, out of date employee benefits are rebroked for cost savings; or a general cost reduction exercise is carried out in the business. Tax reduction can be achieved, but usually through a spending process. For example, pension contributions are tax deductible, and reduce tax, as do other expenditures. However, this spending is offset through **the intrinsic added value** element which is increased. For example, additional pension contributions increase the value of the pension fund and uplifts the value of employees. Purchasing new equipment for the business adds value to the business through say increased productivity and production (which may also add to increased profitability).

Risk Protection is a value attributable to the business which engages in various protection processes. If it did not, this may have an adverse affect on profits. For example, an employee commits a fraud on the business through theft, or the cost of employee tribunals from disgruntled employees; the loss of computer data on which the business depends affects the operations and profitability of the business; a catastrophe affects the business through say fire or floods and it loses production and profits; a key person responsible for sales dies in a car accident, with loss of profits to the business – the list is endless. If the business completes a risk protection audit and takes the necessary steps to limit, prevent or restrict losses to the business, then this is a value factor, adding value to the business. There may be a cost for this, such as insurance, accountants' insurance to pay for losses caused through HMRC investigations, health and safety cover, and so on. However, these are costs well spent, as they aim to prevent business catastrophe.

The Free Cashflow multiplier is a valuation method of similar companies in a business sector. You can divide the price that the acquirer pays for a company by its cash flow, producing a price-to-cash flow multiple. Then you can compare that ratio to the multiple of the company you're looking at. The free cash flow (FCF) multiplier is similar to a price-to-earnings ratio (P/E) because it expresses the value of the enterprise in relation to a single year's performance number. One way of forecasting this number is to look up the current FCF multiplier (current enterprise value divided by most recent year's free cash flow) for this firm, or for other similar firms, and then make subjective adjustments up or down based on beliefs about the long-term or steady-state growth rate that will prevail five years from now.

The most straightforward way for an individual investor to use cash flow is to understand how cash flow multiples work. By looking at recent mergers and acquisitions, you can divide the price that the acquirer pays for a company by its cash flow, producing a price-to-cash flow multiple. Then you can compare that ratio to the multiple of the company you're looking at.

You can either look at sales or profits to determine the multiplier used.

For a sales multiples business valuation methods benchmark used in valuing a business the information needed is annual sales and an industry multiplier, which is usually a range of .25 to 1 or higher. The industry multiplier can be found in various financial publications, as well as analyzing sales of comparable businesses. This method is easy to understand and use. The sales multiple is often used as the business valuation benchmark.

Profit multiples are used for small business valuation benchmarks used in valuing a business. The information needed are pre-tax profits and a market multiplier, which may be 1, 2, 3, or 4 and usually a ceiling of 5.

An example could be a profitable, reasonably healthy, small business that will sell in the 2.0 to 6.0 times EBIT (earnings before interest and tax) range, with most of those in the 2.5 to 4.5 range. So, if annual cash flow is £200,000, the selling price will likely be between £500,000 and £900,000. But there are many factors that affect the multiplier. Some of these are positive, such as lack of competition in the sector, few key people; strong brand, diversified products others are negative – too much competition, too few customers making up much of the sales; products near the end of the life cycle; major investment needed in plant and equipment, and other factors. Positive factors increase the multiplier, negative ones lower it.

Added Value is the immediate and tangible value added as a result of your actions.

Intrinsic Added Value is the immediate tangible and intangible value added as a result of your actions. It may not add value to the business, but to third parties, as a result of your actions – such as the payment into a pension fund benefitting the employees as well as the employer.

Example

Σ (IP + RP) x [M] = AV + IAV

	IP	+ RP	X M	= AV	+ IAV
Before action	£250,000 profits	0 – no risk protection in place	3 x Industry average multiplier (profits)	= £750,000	+ 0
After action	£320,000 increase in profits after cost reduction and tax reduction exercise, including increased pension contributions	£150,000 value of input risk protection after insurance, and tribunal, H & S cover and identifying risk areas	3.5 x Industry average multiplier (profits)	= £1,645,000	+ £30,000
Increase in Business Value				+£895,000 (119% increase in value)	+ £30,000

This company reduced costs and tax, thus increasing profits by £70,000. A pension contribution for employees was made of £30,000 (deductible to the company), which is of great value to the employees. By showing that all areas of due diligence have been covered, overall risk to the company has been reduced. Previously the company suffered 3 employee tribunals in the last year, at a cost of £200,000 in payouts and legal fees. The company identified a rogue line manager who was dismissed, as more employee tribunals were in the pipeline, which were now avoided. A director was uncovered who had been systematically looting the company of an average of £2,500 per month, who was dismissed, and tighter financial controls imposed. The value of risk protection savings to the company was set at a minimum of £150,000. The company industry multiplier average was 3. The company recognised positive aspects in strengthening its management and financial controls, and reducing risk, and this has increased the multiplier to 3.5 x.

The upshot of using the business value formula approach is that it focuses the business on creating value *and proving it*.

This business did not increase sales to more than double its value. It just became smarter and applied business valuation principles through looking inwardly at itself. Reducing risk whilst managing its cost base and undertaking tax – savings wherever possible, has streamlined this business for success.

13

Learning the Numbers

It is important for business owners and those looking to purchase a business to have at least a basic understanding of risk and return analysis and ratios.

Given the business plan of a business, a purchaser must be able to determine whether to invest in it or not. Likewise, a seller must understand what drives and motivates the purchaser, so that adequate planning can take place.

Some basic ratios will act as 'pointers' for your decision-making processes. Compare them with other businesses, usually operating in the same sector.

For example, work out the profitability ratios:

Profit margins

This shows management's use of the resources under its control. Extraordinary items are excluded from this ratio, because they do not represent normal operating profit.

Profit margin = $\frac{\text{profit before taxes}}{\text{sales}}$ x 100

e.g. $\frac{200,000}{2,000,000}$ x 100 = 10%

Return on total assets

Profit is closely related to the assets employed by the company.

Return on total assets = $\frac{\text{profit before taxes}}{\text{total assets}}$ x 100

e.g. $\frac{200,000}{1,300,000}$ x 100 = 15%

Return on owner's equity

This is the return on the owner's capital (equity) investment in the business.

Return on owner's equity = $\frac{\text{profit before taxes}}{\text{owner's equity}} \times 100$

e.g. $\frac{200,000}{750,000} \times 100 = 27\%$

There are literally hundreds of different ratios which can be applied in investigating the performance, liquidity and profit returns for a company, not to mention others which determine what the equity/debt/preference shares investment amounts should be. Whole textbooks have been written on the subject. Serious investors should get to grips with ratio analysis as a constant monitoring tool of what is happening in the business.

The following table is an example of an abbreviated ratio analysis.

Company: ABC plc

	2011	2012
Liquidity/capital structure results		
Current ratio (liquidity 1)	2.6	1.7
Liquidity ratio 2	1	0.6
Gearing (total borrowings against shareholders' funds)	40%	44%
After-tax return on equity	13.3%	8.5%
Pre-tax return on equity	18.3%	15.2%
Returns on total funds	11.4%	10%
Asset turnover	0.9%	0.9%
Net profit %	13%	11.2%
Investigating liquidity		
Sales Increase	–	8.3%
Buys stock	81 days	79 days
Pays debtors	28 days	28 days
Creditor's turnover	28	29
Investigating performance		
Gross profit%	25%	24%
Distribution: sales	5%	4.8%
Administration: sales	7%	8%
Administration increase	–	24%

A quick interpretation of this analysis would show:

- A fall in the liquidity ratio, and the gearing ratio requires a further investigation. Check for new financing and also for working capital increases or decreases.
- Returns on equity falling. If asset turnover has not changed, then investigate the fall in the net profit percentage. In this example, the fall in the gross profit percentage could have resulted from an increase in turnover causing a fall in profit margins. Also the 24% increase in administration expenses could explain the fall in the net profit percentage.
- Tax charges have risen, although profit has fallen. Check accounting policies.
- Decline of operating profitability mainly through gearing and tax factors, increasing administration costs, but not sales performance.
- The company could seek further financing to improve its liquidity position in the near future and would have to explain its existing borrowings and deferred tax liabilities. Internal tightening up on costs is required in administration. Because of increasing gearing levels, possibly the company should consider new equity finance.

The above is a very limited interpretation and is not intended to be comprehensive, only to supply the necessary indicators on how to analyse the figures.

Learn the important ratios for investors

One of the most important ratios for shareholders is to ensure that their dividends are safe, and to achieve this they need profits compared with the dividends payable (dividend cover):

Profit for the financial year = e.g. 120,000 = 2.03
Dividend payable = 59,000

The company could pay the dividend another 2.03 times which should give comfort to investors.

In addition, investors would want to know what the earnings per share will be. It indicates total earnings (dividends plus retained reserves for expansion) which each share generates. Companies strive to increase earnings per share each year.

Take, for example, a company with £100,000 x £1 shares:

Profit for the financial year = e.g. 120,000 = £1.20
Number of issued shares = 100,000
Here, £1.20 is earned for every share held by shareholders.

Learn the 'numbers' and become familiar with ratios. This is all part and parcel of the understanding of the value(s) of the business, an important component in the succession planning process.

14

Identifying Successors

The essence of succession planning, as understood by most people, is to make sure that there is an infrastructure in place for those who will survive the departure of an individual, possibly to replace a key position, or to take over and run the business, and to provide a mechanism to ensure that this happens smoothly.

Previous chapters have focused on preparing the business for departure or sale and maximising its value. Succession planning in the larger, more macro context, was about building the business to a level and value where a smooth business exit could eventuate.

However, there may be more immediate and often crucial decisions to be made in respect of non-sale situations. What happens if a key individual dies, becomes incapacitated so that he cannot work, or is enticed away to another job? What is the position for someone who is promoted from one key position to another – who will take his or her place in the organisation? What if retirement age is reached and the individual is going to leave the business? What if a number of key people want to leave at the same time?

All of these events happen every single day. I was consulting to a progressive firm of lawyers on business planning and the retirement matrix showed 11 partners as follows:

3 Partners (high fee earners) – due to retire in 3-5 years
4 Partners – due to retire in 6- 10 years
4 partners – due to retire in 11+ years

There was no succession plan in place. Who would take their places? How will their pensions and capital accounts in the business be paid out? Partners are the fee earners and life blood of the firm. This firm employed over 200 people, many of whom could lose their jobs in the future.

An advertising agency with major national accounts suddenly lost two key account holders and their teams – they had been poached by a rival firm, and departed almost immediately. Their particular clients would follow immediately. How are they to be replaced? How are their clients to be replaced?.

Tim was a popular member of the sales team in a publishing company. He had a way about him that just brought in the clients and the orders and he accounted for nearly 50% of the new revenue to the firm each year. Tim died whilst taking a well-earned break, trekking in the Himalayas, following his first love of walking and climbing. Who will replace Tim? Tim was married to Morag and had two small children, aged 5 and 7. How will Tim's income be replaced, to enable this family to continue living?

Richard, Gwyn and Iain were fed up. They had been with the same company for a combined total of over 30 years. Yes they received salary increases each year, but no one had ever spoken to any of them about career advancement. Or about their futures as employees. They did not feel valued. 'There might be better prospects elsewhere – where they care about us'. It is not just about focusing on the needs of the organisation, but also about the people in it.

In actual fact, taking each of the above scenarios into account, the main feature is that there is no plan of action in evidence anywhere to cope with any of the above situations. This is often typical of 'working in the business' as opposed to 'on it'. You are too busy to plan ahead. You become even busier when the unexpected consequence affects you.

From the perspective of the organisation, then, succession planning is about the future of the organisation. From the individual's perspective it is about his or her future. After all, the organisation can make the best plans in the world, but if it does not interest the person aimed at, for whatever reason, they are back to square one. It goes without saying then that the business and the individual must be fully aware at all times what the plan is. This enables both parties to adequately prepare for it.

Career paths

The ability to create career paths is critical to the organisation. The business would wish to attract the best talent and to retain them. Management must offer opportunities to retain the best people, and top stop them from leaving, or going to competitors.

Create a roadmap of future leaders

Identifying the future leaders in any organisation takes into account those who have the potential to lead and manage the business, as well as to face the challenges it may have to deal with.

Succession planning focuses on identifying employees who can be developed to take on bigger and more demanding roles in the business. This must be done as early as possible, and must be part of the business's strategic needs. For large businesses this is a accomplished through the HR department; for smaller businesses, management, including business owners will play an important part.

Indeed, if there is not seen to be a leadership pool that can lead the business in the future, it may be the situation that external candidates need to be identified who have specialist talents to take the business forward.

Future succession planning focus has moved away from the needs of the organisation only to incorporating the needs and aspirations and career plans of employees as well. To be successful, you must know your people and understand where the business is going in the short, medium, and long term.

The drivers in the business

The following are best described as the drivers to motivate the need for adequate succession planning.

1. There must be support from the top down in the organisation.
2. The proposition must be communicated to the talent pool and employees, who must be informed.
3. A review should be conducted of both the succession planning strategy as well as the available pool of talent.
4. The board or senior management of the business should give their views on where the business is going and performing and what the leadership challenges will be.
5. Identify the future leaders of the business and its management.
6. Create a programme of activity with training, mentoring and developing core competencies.
7. Review the senior roles in the business, and how these roles would develop in the future. Determine early on if succession will be home grown or imported into the business and when.

Differentiate between leadership and management

What is leadership and how does it differ from management?

Management relies on planning, organisation and communications skills. Skills are first, and not all managers, who are very good at what they do, wish to be leaders. They are quite happy in their management roles, with its laid down and expected competencies.

Leaders should have the necessary skills, but they are about behaviour and attitude. Good leaders are respected and followed by employees because they trust and respect these individuals. Skills are usually secondary. Leadership relies on qualities such as compassion, wisdom, determination and integrity. Aspiring leaders need to focus on strategic thinking, communications, team dynamics, their own self awareness, and interpersonal skills development. Aspirant leaders with potential should be mentored by established leaders with experience, who can pass on these leadership skills and behaviours at first hand.

The importance of technology is not to be underestimated. In managing human capital in the development of succession planning, it can help identify the best performers and those with potential. Technology enables career paths to be tracked, and feedback to be given on progress.

Expectations must be managed. Just because an employee is a high performer, does not mean he will automatically be included in the potential leadership pool. You may be a good manager, but a poor leader. Nothing should be automatic – you still need to win your spurs by demonstrating the ability to lead, develop and create strategies for success.

I worked in an organisation once that was very sales driven. Often the top sales people would be moved into more senior management positions, and those requiring leadership. Many were patently unsuited to management and leadership roles and the organisation suffered as a result – as did their sales, through losing a top producer.

Investing in the business's talent

The business must be committed to developing talent. This must be communicated to all who are engaged in the succession planning process – the plan must be shared with other employees to engage them on where the business is headed. The organisation must invest in its talent pool through leadership development programmes, and commitment to career development. There must also be commitment to retention strategies. This may involve specific benefit packages and lock-ins to prevent the pool of talent from going to competitors. It is therefore important to keep current with market conditions and competition.

Implementing a successful succession plan

Talking about succession planning is one thing, implementing a successful plan is quite another. The Managing Director/CEO of the business will have a business strategy that is communicated to senior management, who, in turn, communicate this to lower management levels. Future needs are critical in this exercise. It means the business must identify where it is now, and where it expects to be within given time frames. Where there are HR departments, their job will be to assist with communication and successor identification.

Every business will have areas that are strengths, and other areas where they may be weak, and an audit of the skills within the business can dictate a plan that requires action, focusing on areas for improvement. How can you move forward efficiently, unless you have investigated those areas that need to be improved?

Once the business's successors have been identified, obtain regular feedback on those individuals, at all times confirming they have the potential to grow and develop into future leaders.

It is important to have a system to measure performance of the individual, and that those performance objectives are closely aligned with business objectives. Involve aspirant leaders in making presentations to the management team to give them experience and exposure at higher levels. Individuals can be coached and mentored to help shape their future leadership ability.

The above describes the need for identifying successors for any business, to create the future leaders for tomorrow.

However, not all succession planning is about developing the next layer of management with leadership skills. This assumes that the organisation has time on its hands, and is able to evolve a gradual process, with training and mentoring to develop future business leaders. This holds true for any larger business organisation.

Smaller Businesses

Whilst the general principles described above are common to all businesses, often the succession planning becomes more immediate, and the planning is immediate. For example, a key person in a small business dies, becomes incapacitated, leaves the business, or retires (without planning) – what then?

If the business has immediate succession covered, and a suitable individual can take the place of the departed key person, then this is not a problem.

However, the loss of a key manager, leader, sales person, for a smaller business could be catastrophic. The business will certainly suffer financial loss, and replacement costs could be high.

Succession planning in this scenario is not just about replacing the person and the value he or she brings to the business, but also replacing the lost revenues to the business, and restoring its profitability.

Succession planning as a main strategy

Whether the business is large or small, succession planning is a main strategy. As a strategy it is dealt with on two distinct levels. One is internal to the business and the development of future leaders. In a different context, succession planning is also linked to business exits, on the sale of the business, for example, and who will succeed to the business overall. This is applicable to smaller businesses, and is absolutely crucial for wealth creation for the business owners.

Part of the business succession plan for the smaller business is to identify leader successors, but another part is to build the business towards a successful business exit. That may entail the identification of a CEO/Managing Director successor to take over the running of the business, or a willing purchaser of the business. Both involve general succession planning principles, in respect of identification of a successor, which may be from within the organisation, or recruited externally.

Who is involved in the succession planning process?

For larger Businesses:

* CEO/Managing Director and Board
* Stakeholders
* HR department
* Senior management
* Outside agencies

For the identification of leaders, as well as successors if a key person is promoted or leaves the organisation. Inherent in bigger business succession planning strategy are longer processes, mentoring and training.

For Smaller Businesses

* Business Owners, including shareholders, partners
* Senior management
* Outside agencies

To replace a key person who leaves, retires or dies; to link business exits with succession planning. Identify leaders as successors, but also other potential business owners.

The thinking is often very different when comparing a larger PLC for example, with a smaller business. This is also case when considering the reasons why business building occurs. The larger PLC business builds profits for shareholders. Usually the CEO/MD of the business has no direct stake in the business (apart from share options), and certainly will not have a majority equity share in it (there are a few exceptions, though). The loss of a key person may not be as acutely felt as a smaller business. For the smaller business, the CEO/MD will probably be a majority business owner, or may even share in the equity, along with other business owners. Their main objective will be to build value and to ensure a successful business exit. Their pool of available talent is smaller for succession planning purposes. Their ultimate succession plan will be to have a successful business exit, with the wealth that may bring them.

For the larger business, personal succession planning for the individual is to have a career path and to personally retire successfully. The business continues with or without them. For these reasons, whilst the focus on succession planning is more internal and longer term for larger businesses; for the smaller business, it may be more immediate and can impact on the future viability of the business.

Taking this a step further – what of the family-owned business, in the past reliant on family members to take over the business (whether good leaders or not)? Their succession planning has been to keep the business in the family at all costs. However, modern reality will focus on their succession planning as identifying future leaders, possibly externally, to continue the business. The family members will still own the business, but create a leadership and management function for a non family member.

Some types of businesses have different succession planning issues. To be a business owner in a legal or accountancy practice, or a medical or dental practice, you need certain qualifications. Whilst this has been watered down for the legal and accountancy professions (who can now have a certain number of non solicitors or non accountants as partners), the succession issues on the retirement, death or departure of a partner are complex. For example, to succeed as a partner, you may have to bring in capital to the partnership. This may limit possible successors.

However, all of the above are still businesses, and they need to be managed and have management teams, and the development of managers and leaders to run the business. The general principles of succession planning with regard to identification, career path development and mentoring apply equally to them.

Our focus is on the smaller business, there being some 4- 5 million of these in the UK today, where succession planning issues are of prime importance, for the protection and smooth continuance of the business, as well as building and preparing the business and its business owners (and possibly employees) for successful business exits.

15

Critical Influences for Succession Planning

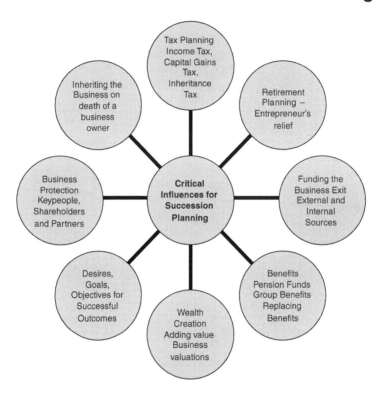

As seen previously, succession planning is a major strategy for large and small businesses. It ensures a smooth transition and an infrastructure for the heir apparent to survive the departure, and provides a mechanism for the smooth transfer of ownership post death or post departure. Identifying successors and leaders is one thing, but planning around the loss of a key person, and protecting the business is quite another.

The underpin for successful outcomes in respect of your objectives and goals for the business and the people in it needs to be planned for. The business plan provides the basis for setting goals and objectives for business owners and the people in the business, and these will need to be prioritised.

For all businesses, the most important element is to protect the business. If the business fails, for whatever reason, there is the loss of livelihood for the business owners, as well as its employees. Continued viability of the business is crucial. In addition, where business risk prevention measures are put in place, this can also add value to the business. Business protection applies to key people in the business, as well as to shareholders, partners, LLP members and sole traders.

People are in business for a number of reasons. Mostly though, for business owners, it provides an income and an opportunity to create as well as to build wealth. The business is developed for value and profitability and this is shared amongst the business owners. The employee in the business works to retire. He and his family is totally dependant on the business to provide him with his living needs and his career aspirations. He therefore has a stake in making sure that the business succeeds. The better the employee does in the business, the better the business should do. A caring business will ensure that the employee is well compensated for his or her efforts in making the business a success.

Both the employees and the business owners expect benefits from the business. The employee expects a salary and employee benefits, and a career path and personal development. He could benefit from lower-costed group schemes (it is cheaper to be a member of one of these, than to individually purchase the benefits yourself). The employee may even be offered a stake in the business through shares and share options. The business owner or shareholder expects a stream of income, usually in the form of dividends, if a company, but also benefits provided for directors, or partners. Some business owners are also employees and may enjoy benefits at a higher level than non-business owner employees.

The business owner will eventually seek to retire from the business, and needs to plan the business exit, along with adequate succession planning. How the business exit is funded will be of crucial importance, and there are a wide range of choices available, from using the employees to raising external bank funding and selling the business. This brings with it the question of how successful the business exit will be for the business owner. Tax implications and retirement reliefs are important, as is the structure of the business exit. All available tax allowances should be used, such as Entrepreneur's relief, and making use of pension funds.

Planning also takes for the heirs of the deceased, should they inherit the business. This level of succession planning is crucial to ensure that there is sufficient value to pass on, and that the heirs are not left with nothing, as a result of the fire sale of the business, through not having proper planning in place.

These critical influences will play a major part in the succession planning of the business as a whole.

16

Protecting the Business Whilst Building Value

Business protection takes many forms. It may be to protect the business itself, from say a fraud or health and safety issue, or the people in it, who are key to income streams and profitability.

Some of the major business risk areas to prepare for are as follows. By not taking business risk preventative measures, it could result in loss of profitability to the business, or at the very least increased costs. These are some of the main areas of business risk.

Business risk areas

- Poor or loose financial controls. If you fail to spot a fraud on the business, for example, an employee putting his hand into the cookie jar, it could cost you thousands. Watch out for small amounts being taken over a long period of time, excess expenditure on the corporate credit card, use of company assets, and your telephone and internet time. Better management can control this.
- Employee grievances. Ending up in a tribunal because of the harassment of a member of staff by a line manager, for example, is an expensive exercise, and could be prevented through better communication, training and management control. You can insure against this, however better management is required.
- Catastrophe risk. The business premises flooding or catching fire, or structural damage is an example. Insure against this.
- Computer/IT risks. If you lose your client database, or cannot access it, or it develops viruses, could have major implications for any business. Insure against this. Have better IT protections.
- Health and safety risks. Included here are employees who work in dangerous occupations, but also events such as corporate manslaughter (where an employee in the company car (or his own vehicle, but on company business) kills a pedestrian or has an accident and death results. The directors could be held liable for this. Insure against this- Directors and Officers Liability insurance and also Health and safety insurance. Have a health and safety audit to find weak areas for prevention.
- Reputational risk. This is the risk of office affairs becoming public, having to contend with this publicly and the loss of business as a result. Business

policy in respect of what you can do and cannot do.

- Pensions funds. Be careful if also a trustee of the company pension fund, you could be held personally liable for fiduciary and other breaches. Trustees are jointly severally liable. Insure against this. Also, under-funded pension funds could be a huge liability for the business's balance sheet and affect its profitability. Possibly change the pension fund (with the consultation of employees of course).
- Cash haemorrhage. The risk here is that cash is being spent on needless or obsolete purchases. Do a cost reduction audit. Identify what you need and where savings can be made.
- Compliance risks. You may be in an industry where compliance is a major factor. Failure to comply could close down your business or result in fines. Include the HMRC here for failure to pay taxes on time, or tax avoidance. You can insure against HMRC investigations through your accountant.

The above is a sample of business risks that can be managed, avoided or insured for. The cost of insurance is cheap, when you consider what might happen if you did not do anything about it, where a risk could be insured against. There are other more intangible risks, such as the loss of interest from investments that can also be planned for. For example, where does the business invest its money? Are better rates available? The loss of interest could be quite substantial.

For example, a business currently earns less than 0.5% on its money in the bank or money markets. 70% of this money is not required for any purpose, being the reserves of the business. The business could invest into a guaranteed term deposit that pays a balloon interest in say 5-6 years' time at up to 12% per annum growth.

Loss of a key person risk

Some individuals will be key to the business. If a key person was to die, become disabled or incapacitated, then this could affect the business's finances and profits.

The first steps are to identify who the key people in the business are, and then to place a value on their loss. Key people could range from the CEO (who has important business contacts and management experience), to the finance director (who controls the financial affairs of the business) a sales person responsible for key client accounts, which may be lost, an IT person who manages the complexities of the business data base and controls its functions. Some people may be easy to replace, others may take much longer.

Succession planning is not only about creating leaders. It is also about identifying key individuals, who could cause the business loss, should one or more of them not be able to perform their functions in the business anymore.

The next step is to place a value on the loss of the key person. Factors to consider are:

* Is the loss temporary or permanent, and for how long?
* Can the individual be replaced from within the organisation or must someone new be hired? If so, what is the time delay, and the cost of replacement?
* Do you have to plan to pay the key person, if off sick for a long period, for example, as well as someone else?
* What is the effect of the loss of the key person likely to be for the business, in financial terms? For example, profits may decrease by 10% in this financial year.
* Does the business feel a responsibility to pay compensation to the family of the key person to compensate them for their loss?
* As a rule of thumb, most key people can be valued at up to 10 x their salaries or earnings. So, Jeremy, a key salesperson earning £60,000 a year, could be valued at £600,000 if he died and had to be replaced.
* Other valuation methods are 2 x gross profits or 4 x net profits. The loss valuation is largely subjective. If you have actual costings directly affected by the loss, then these are acceptable to any insurer.

The following table can assist you in determining who the key people are to the business and the financial implications of their loss to the business.

Name	(1) £	(2) £	(3) £
1. Effect on profits:			
2. Cost of replacement:			
Locum			
Advertising			
Employment costs			
3. Cost of replacing know-how:			
4. Benefit costs:			
5. Pensions			
6. Annuities			
7. Dependant's benefits			
8. Lost contracts costs:			
9. Work in progress lost (value):			
10. Employee contractual payments:			
11. Loan account in business:			
12. Shares repurchase:			
13. Intrinsic value of employee:			
14. Other:			
Total value of key employee:	£............	£............	£............

Example: Determine the range of coverage required, assuming a Key person with an annual salary of £30,000 and a company with gross profits of £250,000, net profits of £75,000. Actual liabilities are £175,000. The Key person has an impact % of 30% on profits. Cover would then be in the range:

1. £175,000
2. £300,000
3. £500,000 x 30%= £150,000
4. £300,000 x 30%= £90,000

The Key person coverage range is £90,000 to £300,000 in this case. With a view to certainly covering (1) at £175,000, the company will probably choose a figure between that and £300,000. This level of coverage should satisfy the HMRC when allowing premiums as a deduction to the business. (Under the 'reasonable amount' test)

Summarise your action plan as shown:

Key person	(1)	(2)	(3)
Method 1:	£............	£............	£............
Method 2:	£............	£............	£............
Method 3:	£............	£............	£............
Method 4:	£............	£............	£............
Choice:	**£**		

Insuring the key person

There are three main types of conventional Key person cover:

- Life cover (to cover against death – usually term cover)
- Critical illness (and disability) cover
- Permanent health insurance (protects against loss of income) cover

There is a further type of disability cover – Key person business expenses cover which is unconventional in that it covers *all* business expenses.

Businesses usually consider Key person life cover (which is really death cover!) as the priority, but more businesses are including health protection cover and disability cover as well.

Problems for the business often arise when a Key person (or any employee for that matter) becomes incapacitated and expects to be supported by the business, which has the additional costs of replacing that person whilst the business income is probably falling.

If a Key person suffers a 'living death' and is critically ill (and incapable of earning), there could be major consequences for the business, family and medical expenses needs. You need more income, not less.

Selecting the right kind of life policy

You have a choice between variations of term assurance or whole of life cover.

If for a short period-up to five years – then select term cover. For longer periods, select renewable term (you can continue with the same cover, an increased premium and no medicals) or convertible term (the option to convert term to whole of life).

For even longer periods use term or whole of life maximum cover, the latter being similar to an 'open- ended term policy'.

Make your key person policy tax deductible

Term policies of five years or less, with a reasonable sum assured, which are not renewable nor convertible, and where the life assured has no substantial interest in the business (between 0% and 5% of the shares) will make the premiums payable tax deductible.

Policy proceeds

Term policies owned by a company have their proceeds taxable.

Whole of life policies owned by a company have tax free proceeds, but the policy gain, which is the difference between the surrender value and premiums paid, is taxable.

If the company owns a term policy, the proceeds are taxable. To achieve true coverage, you then need to increase the sum assured by between 20% and 23.75% (Corporation tax rate to 31 March 2014) to provide for the tax payable.

Proceeds on company owned term policies are taxable whether the premium is tax deductible or not. There is no 'nexus' between the deductibility of the premiums and the taxability of the policy proceeds. However, it has been known for some tax inspectors to allow the proceeds as a tax free amount in the past. The solution is to have the policy in trust outside the company, especially if longer than a five year term, or if renewable or convertible. Premiums come from increased salary paid by the business. Salary is tax deductible to the business. Although National Insurance contributions are payable in the increased salary, this cost is less than the cost of any taxable proceeds. Increased salary also incurs increased pension funding as the salary on which pension contributions are based is higher.

To ensure premiums are tax deductible, get it in writing from HMRC

If the company-owned term policy qualifies for premium tax deductions, get in writing from the HMRC. This only applies to a term policy of five years or less, which satisfies the conditions. Company owned whole of life premiums are *never* tax deductible.

Cost of term (life) cover at various ages and terms

Assume a male, non smoker, with key person term policy and cover of £100,000
Premiums payable per month. Maximum to age 65.

Age	Term 5 yrs	Term 10 yrs	Term 15 yrs
35	£6.40 per month	£6.90	£7.40
45	£10.55	£12.80	£14.70
55	£22.50	£30.60	–

From the above table, a 35 year old key person could obtain £100,000 term life cover for £6.40 per month premium for 5 years. Premiums are guaranteed not to change, and life cover amount is guaranteed not to change.

For a 55 year old, 5 year key person term cover costs £22.50 per month to age 60 and £30,60 per month to age 65 for £100,000 worth of cover.

Note that only term cover for 5 years or less which is not renewable or convertible will be deductible for premiums to the company. Deductible premiums will reduce the cost of the cover even further.

Critical illness protection cover

Assume a male, non smoker, with key person term policy and cover of £100,000.
Premiums payable per month. Maximum to age 65.

Age	Term 5 yrs	Term 10 yrs	Term 15 yrs
35	£13.88 per month	£16.33	£17.66
45	£43.58	£56.64	£67.65
55	£88.36	£101.72	–

Premiums and sum assured are guaranteed.

Policy proceeds are payable on diagnosis of a dread disease or critical illness, such as cancer, stroke, paraplegia etc. Payouts can be paid to the individual or to the company.

Income Protection

Assume earns £50,000 p.a. Deferred period 3 months.

Age	Term 5 yrs	Term 10 yrs	Term 15 yrs
35	£16.80 pm for £25,000 annual benefit rising to £90.44 pm for £124,992 annual benefit	£16.85 pm for £25,000 annual benefit rising to £100.13 pm for £124,992 annual benefit	£20.74 pm for £25,000 annual benefit
45	£24.41 pm for £25,000 annual benefit, rising to £142.13 pm for £124,992 annual benefit	£32.69 pm for £25,000 annual benefit rising to £156.92 pm for £124,992 annual benefit	£47.31 pm for £25,000 annual benefit
55	£69.74 pm for £25,000 annual benefit, rising to £265.51 pm for £124,992 annual benefit	–	–

Policy proceeds are payable to the company, should the key person be unable to work due to illness or injury, in this case, after a deferred period of 3 months. Some life offices will only cover 50% of salary as a benefit to the company, others will pay up to £124,992 annual benefit to the end of the term insured for (in this example). This recognises the loss of profits and additional expenses of the business. Premiums are deductible to the business, and proceeds taxable. (The proceeds will be deductible when used as salary or for other deductibles.)

The cost of providing key person coverages need not be prohibitive. For older people it is more expensive. However, the gross cost of providing £100,000 key person life cover for a 5 year term as a percentage of cover is:

For the 35 year old: 0.0008% p.a.
For the 45 year old: 0.0013% p.a.
For the 55 year old: 0.0027% p.a.

This cost is reduced further if deductible to the business.

Business protection is a key component where the business is to be protected on the death, illness and disability of a key person.

17

Protecting the Business Owners and Future Heirs

Business owners could be shareholders, partners (and LLP members), and sole traders.

Where an individual may have a will to dictate where assets are to go, the business must produce its own 'will' in the form of contractual agreements, that the business owners will be parties to. They can then direct where the shares or partnership value will devolve.

Fundamental is to decide who will benefit under this process. Existing business owners may not wish to have the relatives of a deceased or long-term sick or injured shareholder or partner in the business, and would rather see them paid out a cash lump sum for the value of their share. Likewise, a deceased shareholder or partner would have liked his heirs to benefit from his business share for value. However, he or she is no longer in the business, and cannot influence or control events, unless by prior agreement. There are many influences that come to bear on decision-making. For example, if a company has no history of paying dividends, would you wish your heirs to receive company shares, if dependant on income? No, you would prefer them to have cash to invest for income.

Shareholders (even passive ones) have no rights to call for value from a company in trouble. In fact, they will always be last to get any value – known as distribution dividend, if there is one. The fact of the matter is that unquoted company shares are generally unmarketable and all the more so if anything happens to the company. They are classed as higher risk, and may end up having little or no value at all. Other shareholders may not wish to purchase the shares, or have the finances to do so, even if they did.

Partnerships are even more vulnerable. On the death of a partner, in the absence of any agreements, the 1890 Partnership Act takes over by default. This means that the heirs of a deceased partner have an immediate call for cash for the value of the deceased partner's share. This could spell serious financial trouble for the surviving partners. The other consequences would be as for a company if the partnership failed to survive. LLP members are in much the same position as partners, but the LLP can continue without the LPP member. However, the principles are similar.

Perhaps the most vulnerable is **sole proprietor, or sole trader**. His business usually dies with him. In addition, his employees would have statutory redundancy claims against his estate; in other words, his employees 'inherit' something before his family and heirs. Adequate succession planning is therefore vital for all businesses, large and small. The following strategies will guide you along the correct commercial paths in making a proper 'will' for your business.

Ensure you have key person cover

Providing adequate cash at the right time gives the business financial 'breathing space' whilst it sorts out and implements succession planning objectives, Key person cover is a vital component here.

Develop your succession planning objectives

The following list will help you in the decision-making process:

1. If anything happens to you, such as death or incapacity, what are your plans for the business?

2. If misfortune befalls other shareholders or partners, would you like the following to occur?
   - shares pass to their heirs
   - shares pass to you
   - shares pass to management and/or employees
   - business buys back shares
   - business is sold
   - share pass to surviving shareholders or partners, with cash paid to heirs

3. Who can run the business effectively? Have people earmarked as successors, or must someone be brought in to be a successor?

4. What would you like to happen on retirement?
   the business is sold
   - MBO/MBI (managers to buy the business)
   - employees buy the business (but may not have the means to do so)
   - new shareholders come in to the business
   - business ceases as there is no one able to continue with it

If a sole trader, insure for estate liquidity

Because you are the business, you need to protect your estate and heirs, business liabilities and debts – including salaries owing – as all of these expenditures could come from your estate. Alternatively, consider incorporation (forming a company) to protect your personal wealth.

If a sole trader, have a buy-and-sell agreement with another sole proprietor

Unfortunately, the value of your business dies with you – unless it can be sold for reasonable value after your death. The strategy is to find someone with a similar business in the same position as you. Enter into a buy-and-sell agreement for the other party to purchase your business on your death or even retirement. The parties insure each other to provide the cash to make this sale possible. An example is a pharmacist in one town entering into this arrangement with a pharmacist in another. With a Buy-and-sell agreement A *must* purchase from B.

If shareholders or partners /LLP members then consider a 'double option' agreement

A double option or cross option agreement overcomes the problem of finding cash to purchase the deceased's shares and at the same time gives shares to those who want them (the survivors) and provides cash for those who require this (the heirs of the deceased).

It is also a useful, flexible device to control who gets what in terms of business value and when. Because this is an agreement between the parties, there should be a smooth transaction on death or even disability.

To ensure that cash arises when it is needed, the parties usually insure one another (or take out a life policy and assign it to a trust), with the sum assured paying out to the survivor. The heirs have the *option* to call for cash from the survivors, and the survivors have the option to call for the deceased's shares. Whoever triggers the option must expect the other party to perform. If neither party acts, then the status quo remains with the heirs keeping the shares, the survivors the cash.

This type of agreement is one of sale *after* death and *may* happen – if the option from either side is activated. Consequently the shares fall outside the inheritance tax net.

A Buy-and-sell agreement is similar, but is regarded as a contract for pre-sale and may lose business property reliefs on death and incur IHT liabilities. Here, the parties *must* act and exchange shares for cash.

Examine existing buy-and-sell agreements

If you have a buy-and-sell agreement in place, then perhaps a double option agreement will be more effective or tax efficient for you. Each type of agreement has its place. However, the future loss of business property reliefs for Buy-and-sell agreements has caused a switch to double option agreements over the years, where business property relief on death is not lost.

Older existing agreements may be out of date, as well as levels of cover.

The agreement should have a clause allowing for updating as the value of the business changes.

Check types of life cover and other forms of cover

Life cover is the most popular. However, incapacity, disability or critical illness may have the same effect on a business as death. Modern agreements often incorporate a clause allowing the incapacitated shareholder or partner to buy back his shares after recovering from a heart attack or other critical illness. Many life policies incorporate disability cover and should be considered. On average, you have, at age 40, a one in eight chance of suffering a critical illness before age 65 rather than dying.

For maximum flexibility, include Key person cover above the line with Shareholder or Partner cover

Usually the business takes out the Key person policy, pays the premium (which may be deductible) and the business receives the policy proceeds. These will be taxable in full if a term policy; tax – free if a whole of life (although any gain is taxable – this is the difference between the premiums paid and the surrender value).

The shareholders or partners take out the shareholder protection policies on each other's or their own lives and pay the premiums. These premiums are usually (unless existing pension term policies, which are not available any more) not tax deductible to them for the premiums, but the policy proceeds are tax free. For maximum efficiency and flexibility, combine the two sets of covers. If three shareholders have, say, £100,000 shareholder protection cover and also £100,000 Key person cover, there will be six policies with six separate policy charges. Combining policies reduces these charges by 50%.

Previous Position

Three shareholders or partners, also keypeople,
with separate cover

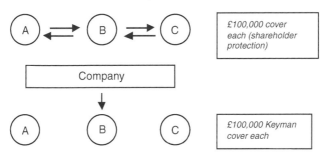

New Position
As above, but with combined cover
Assume C dies

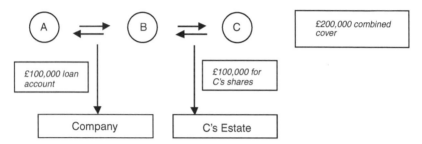

- A and B receive £200,000. Of this, £100,000 goes to C's estate to purchase C's shares. The Key person cover remains, as £100,000 tax-free cash, in the hands of A and B. They can then evaluate the position of the business after the loss of C and:
- Pay cash into business by way of directors' or partners' loan accounts. (loan accounts can be withdrawn an any time. Cash entering the business in this way is not taxable)
- Keep the cash if the business does not need it
- Pay more of the cash to C's estate or dependants.

Each business must assess its own position. The combination Key person and shareholder/partner protection arrangement can be included in the Double Option or Buy-and-sell Agreement.

Cost of Cover

Assume A is a male 2.5.1961; B is a female 7.11.1956; C is a male 24.9.1963. All are non smokers. Sum assured: Term cover to age 65 for £200,000 each, with guaranteed premiums and sum assured; with waiver of premium benefit.

- Cost for A: Life cover £37.52 per month; Life cover with critical illness cover £216 p.m.
- Cost for B: Life cover £37.54 per month; Life cover with critical illness cover £214 p.m.
- Cost for C: Life cover £32.51 per month; Life cover with critical illness cover £180 p.m.

One can have variations, for example, £200,000 life cover and £100,000 critical illness cover, if cost is an issue.

Holding policies in trust

Life Offices have a full range of trusts and trust documentation and literature available on how to set up polices in a business trust, and the mechanics of how premiums are paid, and policy proceeds accounted for.

It is important that policies are placed into a flexible business trust, so that on death, the proceeds are payable into trust and are thus immediately available to the survivors without probate delays. Whilst the type of trust is usually a discretionary trust that will have periodic and exit charges, it is unlikely that the policy proceeds will remain in trust, but be paid out to the survivors, in terms of their double option agreements and other wishes. Thus few if any tax charges will occur as a result of the trust.

Include employee share scheme trusts, employees and managers in your succession planning

The parties to the share holders' sales agreement may be diverse, or as one-sided as you see fit. Some shareholders may wish to buy but not to sell on death of a party to the agreement- or vice versa.

An excellent method of creating marketability of your shares is to have the trustees of your ESOT (Employee Share Ownership Trust) take out a Key person life policy on your life. When you die, the cash proceeds pass to the trustees, who buy your shares from your estate. In this way, a sales process is set up for the shares to pass to employees and managers.

The company can fund the ESOTs trust. This funding is tax deductible to the company (when the beneficiaries receive a benefit). The trust then pays the premiums on the policy.

Capital passes to the trust, which is tax deductible, from the company or borrowings. The trustees buy shares from the share holders. Marketability in shares is created.

Sales of shares to the ESOT's trust need not all be at once. They can be phased over a number of years. This allows the seller the opportunity to use annual CGT exemptions. Currently these are £10,600 per person in 2012/13. Hold over relief may also be available. By selling shares to managers or employees (or surviving partners or shareholders), one can **create a market for shares** where there would otherwise not be a market for the sale of private company shares, and also ensure that shares are purchased at a fair price on retirement or exit from the business.

The key points to consider are that business agreements are the 'corporate wills' of your business and help develop succession planning for your business (a properly – structured shareholders or partners agreement is like a will for the business), ensuring that your business share goes where you want it to go, and for the right value.

Enterprise Management Incentive scheme (EMI)

The 2012 Budget announced the Enterprise Management Incentive (EMI) share option scheme, to encourage more employees to buy shares in the companies that employ them. The cap on the value of share options is currently set at £250,000 in 2013/14.

Protecting the business and business owners whilst creating instant marketability of shares is surely a major objective in the succession planning process.

18

Using Employees in the Business

The business's greatest assets will undoubtedly be its 'people assets' or human capital. The employees use the business for employment and receive benefits as well as salaries. They may receive training, and could be future leaders. High performing employees expect good rewards from the business, and rewards could include a stake in the business, as well as bonuses and other benefits.

Every astute business owner and manager wishes to motivate the people in the business to perform at higher levels and may offer incentives to do so. They also wish to retain their staff, and will have retention strategies in place.

The main question though, is can employees benefit from the business sale, and how do they do this? Secondly, can the business owner use his employees to help with the business exit?

The answer to both questions is in the affirmative.

A company could make available shares or share options to employees, based on performance. The employees could be members of a SAYE scheme, whereby savings are made to purchase shares at a set option date. The interest or bonus on these savings accounts is tax free (even if not used for this purpose, but approved for it). Additional shares could be purchased, or if purchased, matching shares could be given to the employee. When the company is sold, the shares are bought from the employees, who can make a capital gain. Often the shares are held in an employee benefit trust, and dividends can accrue to the employee through the trust.

Alternatively, the business owners could share their spoils through bonus payments to employees.

Partnerships do not have shares, and therefore employee incentivisation is more difficult. However, 'phantom' share trusts can be established, using ISA allowances for employees, or unit trusts for the more forward thinking partnership or LLP. Some partnerships also form a service company to run alongside the partnership, and this company can issue shares to employees and build a valued employee workforce.

The one problem to avoid though is that employees hear about a proposed sale of the business and become nervous about the prospects of new owners and leave the company early on. They should be kept informed at all times, and news of the incentivisation package might increase retention.

Employees helping the business sale

Part of a strategic succession and exit plan is that the business owner(s) or shareholders decide that the employees can fund the purchase of shares from a retiring or exiting shareholder. Usually an employee share trust is established and funded by the company on behalf of the employees, who also contribute to it. Shares are purchased by the trust from the retiring shareholder at a later stage. This route establishes a market for the shares on an internal basis at a pre-determined price. The trust holds the shares for the employees, who have an option to purchase at a later stage.

This route could also fund or assist with funding a management buyout of the shares from retiring business owners.

The trust could also insure the shareholder, so that on death, the shares go to the trust and the estate of the shareholder receives the proceeds. The trust could also be a party to a double option agreement, where it buys shares from any deceased shareholder.

Any contribution to the employee share trust would be deductible to the company against corporation tax, so this is an efficient way to direct funding for a share purchase.

As can be seen, employees can play a major part in the business structure and direction of the business, not only through growing the business, but also through funding new business ownership.

19

Retiring From the Business

The succession business plan for retirement

Your objective is to plan for a successful business exit, having accumulated wealth, planned and implemented your retirement countdown planning, and in the process mitigated inheritance and other taxes.

The twin aspects of accumulating sufficient retirement benefits, savings and investments to retire successfully and exiting the business successfully must be planned for. Retirement countdown planning should begin at least 10 years before retirement, but funding would have started a long time before that.

Those contemplating retirement should be looking to boost their pension funding significantly in the final years up to retirement.

It is important for you to update yourself on how much can be funded into retirement benefits. The pension funding rules are that in 2013/14 you can fund up to 100% of salary capped at £50,000 (with a maximum of £3,600 gross if you have no taxable earnings). There is a lifetime allowance of £1.5 million in 2013/14. Contributions are deductible at your highest tax rates, which could be 45%. Unless your pension fund is registered for enhanced or primary protection, you can take 25% of your pension fund at retirement in tax free cash, known as the pension commencement lump sum. The balance of your funds can be invested and you take an income from the investments within the pension fund. Income levels are capped at between 0% and 120% of GAD rates for all ages. The review period is 3 years. Alternatively you can elect to take an annuity at any time. This annuity income is taxable.

If you are an individual making the funding, pension funding is very tax efficient. Contributions are uplifted by HMRC at the basic rate tax rate of 20% (you contribute £2880, the HMRC adds £720 to make your gross contribution £3,600, for example), and if a higher rate taxpayer, you can have a further 20%-25% currently (at your higher and additional rates of tax) as a return of tax.

Your pension fund grows tax free and the fund itself is not taxed.

For those in occupational pension schemes, there is no HMRC uplift of your contribution (unless you make additional contributions yourself to a separate scheme), and you may take a pre-determined pension from a final salary (defined benefits) scheme and tax free cash. If in an occupational scheme defined contributions (Money Purchase) arrangement, an annuity is purchased to give you a pension, usually. Pension contributions are deductible to the employer.

Retirement choices on what sort of pension arrangements to make can also be planned for now. Will you take a full pension, without any tax free cash, or take the tax free cash and a reduced pension at retirement? Should you take income drawdown or an annuity? The state of your health is a determining factor. If in ill health, or a smoker, you could get a higher annuity rate, and higher retirement pension. Shop around at retirement for the best rates.

Taking tax free cash will enable you to pay off a mortgage, reduce liabilities, buy a new car, or make investments.

It is important in the planning process that you get updated on the pension fund rules and the options available to you.

You can retire from your pension scheme and still carry on working full time, or part time, if you wish to do so (and your employer allows this).

Retirement ages currently from personal arrangements are from age 55. Occupational pension fund rules usually allow you to retire from age 60 or 65.

Retirement is not just about pension funding. It includes taking into account the state pension (currently age 60 for women and 65 for men, but moving towards equalisation and increasing to 68 for both sexes by 2020); your savings and investments, property, and other income sources.

If you do not have a pension scheme

If in a partnership or LLP, the partners can make a pension and lump sum payment to a partner who has not funded for himself. The pension or annuity payable is treated as earned income of the recipient for tax purposes. The partners receive a tax deduction for the payment of the annuity or pension. This type of unfunded pension may be an interesting way of repaying a retiring partner's capital account in instalments, whilst providing tax reliefs to the other partners for doing so. It is essential that the mechanism for paying an unfunded pension be included in the partnership agreement. Do not substitute this method for the more tax efficient pension funding route, but use it where little or no pension funding has occurred.

If a company employee, the company can also make unfunded pension payments. The company can pay benefits out of current income or investments to you. There is no charge to tax for any reserves set up to provide for your future benefits. Tax relief arises for the company when the benefits are paid to you. You will be taxed on the pension received as earned income. An unapproved lump sum will also be tax as earned income.

There are also strategies for companies to set up employer funded employee benefit trusts, that may be more tax advantageous.

Steps in the review process

You need to review your assets and liabilities to determine whether you will have surplus or deficit income in retirement.

Review your Assets

* Value of current pension fund
* Value of other pension funds
* Value of retirement benefit schemes
* State pension benefit forecast (use form BR 19)
* Value of non pension investment assets
* Company shares
* Partnership/LLP capital accounts
* Partnership/LLP share value
* Share of partnership/LLP properties
* Director loan accounts value
* Money owed to you and loans made by you
* Maturing endowment policies and investment bonds
* Assets likely to be sold, let or rented out
* Possible inheritances
* Consultancy or other employment income
* Other assets

Review your Liabilities

* Household expenditures
* Living expenditures, food, entertainment
* Utilities – light, water, gas
* Motor vehicles, fuel and car costs
* Mortgage, rent, nursing home fees
* Council tax
* Insurances
* Holidays
* Gifts
* Cleaning
* Taxes subscriptions
* Second properties
* Life assurance and other premiums
* Medical insurance and medical expenses
* Other

Review your Income

Income now: £

Income expected in Retirement: £

Do the sums – take total cash outflows from income to determine surplus or shortfalls.

It is most important that you have a review conducted for your retirement by a qualified financial planner. This should show you the various options available to you now and at retirement. My book 'Pensions Simplified' also takes you through this process.

The above deals with aspects in relation to your pension fund. However, for business exit and successful succession planning to work, these are the guidelines for retirement.

Companies

If a shareholder, or a director and a shareholder you will own shares and possibly also have a director's loan account in the business.

If a shareholder

You will decide whether to keep the shares or to try to sell them. Factors that may influence you will be whether the company has a history of paying dividends or not; whether the company may be sold at a later date and you will profit from such a sale; whether a market exists for your shares, or other shareholders will offer to buy them. Pricing of privately owned shares is always difficult and usually ends up being the price someone will pay for the shares – not necessarily what they are worth.

If you die in retirement (a likely event at some stage), then what happens to your shares? You can leave them to your heirs, or if there is a buy-and-sell or double option agreement in place, the surviving shareholders will purchase the shares from your estate, the share price having been made available through life assurance. It is therefore important that you remain part of any buy-and-sell of shares arrangement, even after retirement. The agreement would have to be changed to allow you to sell, but not to buy anyone else's shares (unless you wish to do so). Private company shares are usually not liquid assets and may be unmarketable. However, there may be a mechanism in place whereby a share trust for employees could purchase your shares on retirement or death, the trust being funded by the company or employer.

Check the company's articles to see where and when and to whom your shares may be offered for sale. You may find restrictions – for example you cannot sell your shares to an outsider without offering them to existing shareholders first.

If you have a director's loan account

You may have money in the company by way of a director's loan account. The company owes you this money, and on retirement you would wish it to be paid back to you. If you died, there is no business property relief for inheritance tax purposes on director's loan accounts, and this cash could be liable for IHT at 40% currently. The company could borrow commercial funds with deductible interest and repay you.

Leaving the Company

The company could sell you your company car or gift it to you (tax is payable).

Other employee benefits would cease, as you are no longer an employee. However, you could remain as a consultant and receive an income, if this was acceptable to you.

Partnerships and LLP members

Retirement can be a tricky business, if current partnership agreements are anything to go by. You will have a partner's capital account, essentially your tax paid money in the business, as well as a current account, and may also part own a property along with other partners.

Many partnership agreements are not terribly clear on what happens at retirement. Some partnership agreements state that on retirement, the partnership capital account will be repaid in ten equal instalments over the next ten years, which is not satisfactory if planning your retirement. The problem is that your capital account reflects both the value and strength of the business, as well as its working capital. If a senior partner or LLP member retiring from the business, this withdrawal of your capital account could have a marked effect on the cash flows of the business you are retiring from. Again, the partners could replace your capital account with bank funding (and deductible interest), or bring in a new partner who introduces capital into the business.

Be aware of what the partnership agreement says on death, disability and retirement. Many agreements also stipulate that partners and LLP members must be responsible for their own pension funding arrangements and there may not be a partnership pension plan in place.

Other considerations may involve your share of a partnership property, usually used by the business. Paying you out your share of this asset could be problematic, unless there is new blood coming in to the partnership, who is prepared to take it over from you. The same holds true for SSAS or group SIPP pension schemes holding property. The pension scheme must pay you a pension and tax free cash, but this may be difficult if the only asset of the fund is a commercial property. It is better to have a hybrid scheme with insured funds or other funds to enable it to pay pensions when required.

Review your partnership and property agreements to ascertain exactly what the position is. Once you have retired, your influence in the previous business is on the wane and getting through changes will be difficult.

Expect only the value of your capital account and what is left in your current account on retirement. Whilst the business itself may have a high value due to reputation and goodwill and other factors, it is unlikely that this value will come to you, as there is no provision usually to pay you out any enhanced value. The position may be different if the partners have a double option or buy-and-sell agreement to make a death payment to your estate, provided you remained in this business agreement arrangement post death, and continued to pay your premiums.

It is no wonder then that partners and LLP members are seen to be 'in it for themselves' and must accumulate as much retirement assets outside of the partnership/LLP, using the partnership to create wealth.

Partners are jointly liable for VAT owed by the firm up to the date of notification of retirement, not the actual date of retirement, and this liability needs to be addressed when considering retirement.

On retirement, the retiring partner's tax liability is based on a full year's assessment which should raise a residual liability in retirement.

At retirement, part of the partner's capital account is a realised capital gain which is triggered. The partner should ask if there is a revaluation of any previous surpluses as liabilities may arise on past revaluations of partnership assets. The partner may be better off by deferring retirement and dying 'in harness'. If not, then there is a possibility that business property relief at 100% is in danger. If the partner is in ill-health, then consider staying on as a partner and don't retire.

If the partnership has old 'Buy-and-sell' clauses in its partnership agreement, then these must be taken out. Buy-and-sell clauses give a binding contract for pre-sale of the partnership share which would disqualify the partner form business property relief. Rather use a double option agreement which enables the business property relief exemption of 100% from inheritance taxes on death. If the partner is forced to take early retirement or is expelled from the partnership, then the following considerations are important, as they impact on future wealth planning of the partners.

For example, an exit from the partnership may be coupled with a restraint of trade or the payment of a lump sum, or an annuity. There may be a high price to pay if not properly planned. Also, there is no tax relief for the payers of a lump sum. If there is a pay-off, what will be the best route to take? Naturally, one would wish to maximise the net after-tax benefit. If a lump sum is paid to the retiring or expelled partner, then one must look to capital gains tax reliefs.

The partnership and early retiring partner should consider the different implications of paying and receiving a lump sum, or an annuity, or being retained through a consultancy agreement. If an annuity, then entitlement to it should be in the partnership agreement. One should not mix the payment or consideration of an annuity and lump sums together. If so, the annuity could be capitalised and treated in the same way as the non-deductible lump sum.

A consultancy agreement would have to satisfy the 'wholly and exclusively' test for deductibility of the payments under the agreement. This is not the case with an annuity. However, consultancy payments are 'net relevant earnings' for pension contribution purposes, whereas annuity payments are not. One must give equal consideration to the tax position of payers in order to maximise the compensation package. Bear in mind that the exiting partner will require releases from loans, finance arrangements and professional indemnity on retirement, as well as full indemnity against partnership debts.

The retiring partner could still be liable for partnership debts and actions and should retain PI cover for 'run-off' once retired. This is a complicated area and professional advice should be sought to maximise retirement and early leaving benefits from a partnership. If the partnership contemplates a husband and wife situation, or civil partners, this could be useful to obtain greater Entrepreneurs' retirement reliefs. Whist it is generally inadvisable for both spouses to have unlimited liability (perhaps one should be an employee), both have entrepreneur's retirement reliefs. The spouse should be brought in as a partner before disposing of the business, to maximise this relief.

Husbands and wives, and civil partners, are treated separately for Entrepreneurs' Relief. Each person is entitled to relief up to the maximum lifetime limit of £10,000,000 qualifying gains taxed at 10%, provided the relevant conditions are satisfied.

Where you hold shares jointly with another person, whether that is your husband, wife, civil partner or someone else, in deciding whether the company is your personal company you are treated as holding the appropriate proportion of the total holding and associated voting rights. For example, where a husband and wife own the entire issued ordinary share capital of a company jointly, they are each treated as holding 50% of the shares and 50% of the voting rights.

Sole traders

In a nutshell, the sole trader is the business, and when he retires, possibly the business retires with him. This is often the case for more personal service businesses. However, for many the business could be sold as a going concern and this provides a business exit that is profitable.

Continuing liabilities

All businesses that carry current professional indemnity liabilities and insurances, may require the retired person to carry what is commonly known as 'run-off' insurance, to protect them in retirement on the business they conducted whilst working. Failure to do so, could cost you your assets in retirement.

This is also the case for trustees, including pension trustees. Retiring does not end your obligatory duties and you could be jointly and severally liable for the actions of any trustee. This liability is personal to you, and you could lose all of your assets. Make sure, as part of your retirement and succession plan that you have the necessary insurances in place – after retirement.

The same holds true if you have provided guarantees to a bank for example, on the business bank account. Even though you have retired, this does not automatically end the covenants you provided to the bank, and the bank could make a call on you, even though you retired from the business many years previously. Make sure that personal guarantees leave the business when you leave.

It could be that on retirement, the business has been sold. Conditions of sale may require you to continue to service clients during the takeover period, or other 'earn-out' provisions. Make sure that the necessary insurance covers are in place to protect you, during this period.

Retiring from the business may mean simply going off on pension, or it could have wider implications such as selling the business, or appointing successors previously identified by you. You may have lump sums to invest, and would need to ensure that you are making use of tax and other allowances, to ensure as successful retirement as possible.

20

Tax Planning

Tax planning is important at various stages of the succession planning cycle. During the investment process, the individual or business will be seeking to minimise taxes paid, and may use tax-reducing investments and other tax planning.

In this chapter, the main area to be covered is in respect of tax planning around the business exit, and how to accomplish this effectively.

Sale of the business

The general rule is that capital gains tax is payable on any gains made from the sale of the business or business assets. There is two-tier rate structure, with 18% payable on gains and taxable income up to £32,010 and 28% above that, for capital gains tax, after any CGT reliefs that may apply. Each individual has a CGT personal allowance, presently standing at £10,900 in 2013/14. This has risen annually with inflation, and may do so in the future.

If a business is being disposed of, there is Entrepreneur's Relief from capital gains tax on any gains arising. This relief became effective from 6 April 2008. Schedule 3 of the FA 2008 applies.

The relief is available where:

*   Gains are made on the disposal of all or part of a business
*   Gains are made on disposals of assets following the cessation of a business
*   Gains are made by individuals who were involved in the running of a business.

The first £10,000,000 of gains that qualify for relief will be charged to CGT at an effective rate of 10%. Gains above that threshold are charged at 18-28%. The £10 million limit is a lifetime limit and claims can be made more than once, up to that limit.

There is no minimum age limit.

You must have held qualifying assets for at least one year.

The relief does not apply to companies and personal representatives of deceased persons. It only applies to individuals and trustees. Husbands, wives and civil partners are separate individuals and each may make a claim up to the maximum amount, so long as they satisfy the conditions.

The relief does not apply to a property letting business, other than furnished holiday lettings.

The relief applies to gains realised on disposals of the whole or part of a trading business, carried on by an individual or in partnership.

If a business simply ceases, (is not sold), relief is available on the gains on assets formerly used in the business and disposed of within three years of the business ceasing.

If company shares in a trading company are sold, the relief will apply, providing the individual making the disposal:

• Has been an officer or employee of the company (or of a company in the same group of companies)
• And owns at least 5% of the ordinary share capital of the company and has at least 5% of the voting rights in that company

Relief also applies to associated assets used in the company's business. This may be the case where the shareholder owns individually premises let to the company and sold at the same time. The same rule applies to a partner. The asset relief may be restricted if not used wholly in the business.

Trustees can also benefit from similar reliefs on gains on assets used in a business. The beneficiary must have in interest in possession in respect of those assets and must be involved in carrying on the business in question.

Claims for Entrepreneurs Relief are made through your tax return.

Qualifying conditions

• Disposal of a whole or part of a business which you have owned directly, or in a partnership where you were a member – a distinct part of the business must be disposed of.
• Cessation of business – disposal of assets – claim within 3 years
• Company shares – 1 year qualifying period

There are various other qualifying conditions see HMRC helpsheet 275. Often only a proportion of the gain will be allowed for relief, depending on the circumstances.

Example

• Jenny sells her business for £450,000. She owned it for more than one year. She earns £50,000 per annum.
• £450,000 is reduced by 4/9ths(by £200,000) to £250,000.
• £250,000 less the annual exemption of £10,600 = £239,400
• £239,400 x 28% = £67,032 capital gains tax to pay.

Example

Miles is a partner with three others in a trading business. Each had a 25% share in the partnership assets. Miles retires on 31.12.2011 and transfers his 25% interest in the assets of the business to the other partners, who continue to trade. Gains are made of £250,000 on the disposal of the partnership share of the business goodwill and premises. Miles qualifies for 100% Entrepreneurial relief because he has disposed of the whole of his interest in the partnership's assets.

Example

Tony was a shareholder and director in a company for 20 years, and owned 15% of the shares and had 15% of the voting rights. In 2011 he sells the shares and makes a gain of £500,000. The company had been trading, but ceased doing so in September 2010, ceasing to be a qualifying company. Tony will still qualify for 100% Entrepreneurs Relief as the disposal was made less than 3 years after the company ceased to qualify as a trading company.

Example

Freddie is a farmer. He has a life interest in a settlement that owns the farm. There are other beneficiaries and he only gets 25% of the income arising from the farm land. He ceased farming to take retirement, and the trustees sell the farm land. There is a gain of £500,000. He and the trustees jointly claim Entrepreneur's Relief. The trustee's gain that is eligible for relief is restricted to £125,000 because Freddie was only entitled to 25% of the income from the farm land. [£500,000 x 25% = £125,000].

It is important that you keep a record of disposals and gains and how much of the Entrepreneur's Relief was used. This is because there could be more than one disposal in your lifetime, and the cap is set at £10 million worth of gains at the 10% effective rate. The excess is taxable at 18%-28%, depending on taxable income. The claim for Entrepreneur's Relief is under section 169M of TCGA 1992.

Planning areas

1. As both husband and wife and civil partners each have the £10 million maximum Entrepreneur's Relief, and the qualifying period is one year, assets can pass from one spouse to another free of tax and be any gains claimed for maximum relief. If the value of the disposal is less than £10 million, then there is still the additional CGT personal exemption that could have been used.
2. Check your business assets and personal assets used in the business, and during which periods. Realign your assets so as to achieve maximum effect.

3. Valuations are obviously important and can also include goodwill. Make sure that you have considered all aspects in valuing your business, in order to claim maximum reliefs.

Tax Planning around the business exit is crucial. The retirement reliefs from capital gains tax for most people are reasonably benign at between 10% and 28% at present.

Exiting the business – on death

If you die, the value of your business share would pass according to your will or on intestacy. A business asset may be subject to Business Property Relief (BPR) from inheritance taxes. This is available at up to 100% on qualifying business assets/share and 50% for certain farming or agricultural assets/share. You must have held the business asset/share for at least 2 years to qualify for BPR from inheritance tax. However, if you sold the business share prior to death and it represents cash or a similar non-qualifying business asset, then 100% would be dutiable in your estate (less allowances such as the nil rate band, which in 2013/14 is £325,000). Your strategy, if facing IHT issues in relation to your estate could well be not to sell shares in a company, for example, so that they qualify for BPR from inheritance tax.

Entrepreneur's Relief is not available to personal representatives in your estate, so any sales gains arising after death could be subject to capital gains tax at 18% -28%.

On the death of a business owner, where the share qualifies for BPR, the share can pass to another person or trust without inheritance tax being paid. Capital gains tax holdover reliefs are also available, so that CGT can be held over if the gain is reinvested or held in trust until sold or passed to others. Shares qualifying under the enterprise investment scheme rules (EIS), if held for two years, are not subject to IHT.

Death – sole trader

If a sole trader, on death, the business dies with you. The business assets will either be taken by your heirs or sold off. This will probably be at a 'fire sale' or second hand valuation. You may have some value in a book of clients or client contacts that could be sold, but generally the sole trader is the most vulnerable. Your estate may be left with business debts, including the wages of redundant employees. Life cover is the most important succession planning device for the sole trader to protect business assets, as well as for family protection.

Partnership or LLP

On death the value of your share does not pass automatically to other partners (unless there is an accrual clause in your partnership agreement). The following could be the most likely scenarios.

- There is a partnership/LLP agreement to the effect that partnership shares will be purchased by the surviving partners, who will insure each other, so that cash is available to purchase your partnership share. This value is determined by a pre-set formula. The proceeds of the life assurance are paid to your estate or trust. This will be tax free. However, if a buy-and-sell agreement was used, then the proceeds could be liable for inheritance tax. If a double option agreement was used, then no IHT is payable.
- There is a partnership//LLP agreement that states that capital accounts will be paid on death and the value of all partnership/LLP shares will automatically accrue to the surviving partners who do not need to purchase the partnership shares. This will be seen as a capital gain for them, and capital gains tax may be payable by each partner. Your capital account is received by your estate tax free and also has business property relief (BPR), so long as the conditions are satisfied, and no inheritance tax is payable. Your current account would be subject to income tax in the normal way.
- The partnership/LLP agreement states that the partnership share will be paid to the deceased's estate over a period on death or retirement. This is usually ten years. There should be no IHT if BPR applies.
- By agreement, nothing is paid for your share. The accrual method would apply.
- In the absence of agreement, the default position is that the 1890 Partnership Act applies for partnerships and heirs can call for cash for the value of the deceased partner's share.
- On death a partnership dissolves, unless there is agreement to the contrary. An LLP will continue in existence.
- Partnership shares or value will pass by will or on intestacy, unless there is an agreement in place dictating otherwise.

On death, partners are not as vulnerable as sole traders, but have less protection than LLP members, who have limited their liability.

At the very least, for protection purposes, there should be a double option agreement with partnership/LLP life cover as a bare minimum to ensure that fair value for a share passes to the family or estate. Do not forget PI run-off cover if a professional partnership. Claims against the estate or in retirement could have a devastating effect on the family wealth.

Companies and shareholders

The death of a shareholder does not affect the business, unless the company decides to buy back the shares and cancel them (or unless the shareholder was active in the business). The value of his shares falls into his estate, and if a qualifying company, the shares should benefit from business property reliefs (BPR) and not be subject to inheritance tax.

The following are the most common options:

* The shareholder leaves his shares by will, or they pass on intestacy. No inheritance tax if the shares qualified for BPR reliefs.
* The company articles may state that shares must first be offered to other shareholders before being sold to third parties. If shares are sold then capital gains tax may be payable on any gains (and there are no entrepreneurial reliefs if the estate sells the shares).
* Shares could be sold to an employee share trust (ESOT) on death. Capital gains tax may be payable without reliefs.
* A shareholders' agreement provides for life assurance on the shareholders' lives, held in a business trust, so that the survivor shareholders can have the cash to purchase the shares of the deceased. This is usually accompanied by a double option agreement, so that the arrangement is IHT effective.
* The majority of heirs would rather have cash than shares, on the death of a shareholder, especially where shares have a history of paying low or no dividends.

Death of a shareholder is the least vulnerable position for a company. The company can be continued and the shares can be sold.

Investing the proceeds

The first steps in the investment process are to decide on your objectives for investment. Are the investments to provide income, or capital growth or both? How long can you invest for? Do you need to reduce income tax (or other taxes, including inheritance tax), or defer a capital gain without paying capital gains tax?

What is your risk profile for investments? Are you an exceptionally cautious investor, or can you be more adventurous? Then you need to ensure that you do not have all of your eggs in one basket by diversifying your investments. Asset allocation is important here- how your investment funds are to be best allocated amongst different asset classes to spread investment risk. How you invest the proceeds of your business sale, will determine what sort of tax liability you will have on the investment itself, or whether the investment is tax deductible to you.

Investments can be tax reducing, tax deferred or tax free.

Tax reducing investments

If you do not wish to pay any capital gains tax, you can defer the capital gain through investing into an EIS qualifying investment – an unquoted company or AIM stock. The amount of deferment is unlimited and if you make the investment, 30% of up to £1 million can be deducted for income tax purposes as well – and the value of the investment is out of your estate after 2 years for IHT purposes. Income tax already paid can be reclaimed from the previous tax year, using this investment. The new SEEDEIS allows you to claim up to 50% tax relief on an investment of up to £100,000, but that must be backdated to 2012/13. CGT reliefs are however available in 2013/14.

You can defer a capital gain until you die, and then it dies with you. Alternatively, you can reactivate some of the gain each year and utilise your personal allowance, where currently £10,900 per person is free of capital gains tax. Capital gains tax can therefore be an optional tax, which never has to be paid.

You can make tax-reducing investments. These include the EIS mentioned above, and also venture capital trusts (VCTs) that are tax deductible at 30% of the investment made up to £200,000 per person. The investment grows tax free and there is no capital gains tax when you dispose of it. EZ (enterprise zone) or BPRA (Business Premises Renovation Allowance) investments reduce taxable income. The investment is unlimited and around 90% of it reduces your taxable income, and therefore your tax.

For all of the above, you will need a higher risk profile.

Pension contributions as investments

Pension contributions as investments could be a strategy that brings tax relief, if a higher rated taxpayer, plus a guaranteed return from HMRC of 20% on each contribution made.

The fund grows tax free and if age 55, you can take 25% of the pension fund investment in tax free cash and the balance will pay you a guaranteed income for life.

You can make annual single premium deductible pension contributions into a personal pension plan. Each year, you can take out the tax-free cash element (25% of the fund) and use this for income. The balance of your fund is available to purchase a pension, most of which can be deferred until actual retirement date. The total tax relief for a higher rated taxpayer is 20% and for additional rate taxpayers 25% on the contribution plus an HMRC contribution of 20% to the pension fund. In addition, 25% in tax-free cash is available *for each* single premium pension payment made each year. You could have over 30% in guaranteed returns through taking tax free cash from a Pension Fund and having an income paid for life. If a 40%-45% taxpayer, you get an additional 20-25% tax relief on your contribution, thus reducing the net cost of the investment even further. The maximum contribution is capped at £50,000, and if in employment, this income includes the value of employer contributions.

Example

What if your income is so low you don't have to pay tax? Then your maximum pension contribution is capped at £3,600 per tax year. But you only actually need to contribute £2,880 to achieve a pension pot this size. This is because you still benefit from 20% basic-rate tax relief – so you effectively get a £720 contribution from Her Majesty's Treasury.

Furthermore, if you are aged over 55, then you can immediately withdraw a quarter (25%) of this pot as tax-free cash. In other words, you can get back £900 of your £3,600 straight away. So, after deducting the £720 tax relief and tax-free cash of £900, a pension contribution of £1,980 nets you a pension pot of £2,700.

You then use this £2,700 pot to buy a pension annuity – a guaranteed income paid by an insurance company until you die. You can choose to have this annuity income paid yearly in advance, which means that you can get your first year's payment straight away. Total guaranteed returns over 30%, every time you use this strategy.

Tax free investments

You would make use of your ISA allowance, which is £11,520 per person per year. This investment grows tax free, and on encashment there is no capital gains tax to pay. It is also instantly accessible.

There are two investment components – cash, and stocks and shares. You can invest the whole £11,520 annual allowance into stocks and shares each year; or £5,760 into cash, and £5,760 into stocks and shares. You must be aged 18 or over to have an ISA (except for age 16 for a cash ISA, or any age for a Junior ISA to age 18).

Other investments that grow or mature tax free are certain National Savings products; Friendly Society Investment Policies; MIPS and endowment policies; Forestry Investments; Pensions; Spread bets/FX trades; Personal Annuities (where the capital element is tax free).

Tax deferred investments

These investments may have tax free income now, but tax could be payable later, depending on your circumstances.

Investment bonds

These are single premium life assurance policies invested into a wide range of funds and asset allocation classes as selected by you. Each year, the investor could withdraw 5% of the investment 'tax deferred'. These 5%'s are cumulative, so if you don't withdraw anything for, say, 10 years, then you can take 50% out of the bond without any tax charge at that time (10 x 5% = 50%). Tax deferred means that if you are a basic rate taxpayer at maturity of the bond, no further tax is payable – if a higher rate taxpayer, you pay a 'top slice' of income tax as an additional 20%-25% amount of tax.

There are other tax advantages for investing into an investment bond – some are used to reduce immediate inheritance tax in your estate through a discounted gift trust (this may be appropriate for parents or grandparents). Offshore investment bonds have 'gross roll up' meaning the investments in the bond are not taxed during the growth period. There is no capital gains tax to pay at any time. At surrender or maturity, income tax may be payable, depending on your tax status and residency in the UK or not. However, always compare investment bonds (income taxed) with unit trusts and OEICs which are subject to a much lower capital gains tax rate of 18%-28%.

Investment bonds have a wide choice of funds and investments and you can be conservative or adventurous as you please; you can switch investments within the bond, as your circumstances change.

The bond on encashment is subject to income tax. The tax treatment differs depending on whether the bond is an onshore or an offshore bond.

Gains for onshore bonds: if you are a basic rate taxpayer at maturity – there is no further tax to pay. If a higher rate taxpayer, then tax is payable at the higher marginal rate less the basic rate, at present 40 – 20 = 20% up to £150,000 and 25% if above that. The funds in the bond itself are taxed annually and there is no gross rollup applying.

Gains from offshore investment bonds are taxed as income at 20% or 40% (rising for some to 45% in 2013/14). The main advantage is that the one can obtain gross rollup on the investments within the bond during its term (and not be taxed during the term).

Deposit accounts with deferred interest

Some bank accounts and some investments allow you to defer interest. You only pay tax when the interest is received.

Capital gains investments

Tax efficiency can be obtained through using investments that produce capital gains.

For individuals the tax rate for capital gains is 18-28% depending on income. For taxable income and gains up to £32,010 the rate is 18%, above that it is 28%. There is a flat rate of 28% for trusts.

Individuals each have a CGT exemption of £10,900 in 2013/14.

Trusts have an exemption of half that rate of £5,450 (split between up to 5 trusts).

Many investments provide for capital gains as opposed to taxable income. A married couple could have £21,800 in this tax year as tax free 'income' from capital gains. Investments that produce capital gains are unit trusts and OEICs, for example, or second hand endowment policies.

Making use of your allowances – taxable investments

You may have income taxable investments, however your personal allowances would render all or part of them tax free.

Personal allowances for 2013/14 are as follows:

Under age 65:	£9,440
65 -74:	£10,500
75 and over:	£10,660

Age related allowances are progressively withdrawn if taxable income exceeds £26,100.

Your investment strategy is important, but so are taxation considerations, so that you keep more of what you make. Your succession planning at the time of business exit will include investment and tax planning. There are many different areas to think about. One of these is that the sale price for your business could include making an investment such as a large pension contribution on your behalf when you exit the business. You can have up to £50,000 as an annual allowance or 100% of salary if lower, and can also carry forward unused allowances for 3 years – but must have had a pension scheme during those years of carry forward.

21

Funding the Business Exit

Deciding to sell the business and actually structuring the business deal that makes it happen takes a lot of planning. Every conceivable sales route should be examined, and with it the sales price that it might bring. For example, if selling the business to management and employees- would you expect the same price than if you sold the business by way of trade sale or to third parties?

Some routes may result in an easy sale, others may be more difficult. Some routes may involve a partial sale (of say one shareholder only), or the whole business. It must be decided what is to be sold and at what price, following a fair valuation.

For companies

The following will be the most likely purchasers:
* Selling to existing shareholders or stakeholders
* Using your employees and/ or managers to buy the business
* Using management to buy the business
* Selling to third parties, trade sales
* Selling to venture capitalists or private equity concerns
* Selling to VCTs
* Listing the company on Plus, AIM or the main stock market

The following are the most likely sellers:
* Shareholders or partners/LLP members
* Deceased estates holding shares
* Heirs holding shares
* Trusts holding shares
* Pension funds holding shares
* Private equity or venture capital firms seeking an exit
* Venture Capital Trusts (VCTs) seeking an exit

Funding the sale/purchase of shares

If individuals, trusts and third parties they would use their own cash or arrange loans to make the purchase. If employees and management, bank finance would be arranged, usually using a mix of company assets and personal assets as security for finance to do so. Pension funds, venture capital trusts, private equity firms and venture capital firms will use their own finance.

In certain instances, to assist with the sale, the seller may even make loans (issue loan notes), and arrange for the buy-out finance to enable the sale to proceed successfully.

The sale price make-up needs to be determined at an early stage. It could be a mix of cash, loan notes, shares in the acquiring company, bank finance and trade finance. It could even be payments to a pension fund for an individual, made as part of the sales price.

Whilst the business owner may have certain ideas, the earlier discussions begin with likely sources of finance and interested parties, the better the deal could be.

If a partnership or LLP

Buying a share in a company is much easier to fund than a share of a partnership. This is mainly because of security issues in respect of what is being bought. A company share can be used as security, however a partnership share can't be so used. The assets of the partnership can be securitised though, and liens can be taken on capital accounts.

The sales process is more subjective, as the business is more or less the people in it, and their endeavours (for professional partnerships, such as solicitors, doctors, architects, or personal service partnerships, such as IT consultants).

The person buying the partnership share becomes a partner, and may need to be qualified in the profession to become a partner. He or she will usually have to take out a loan or remortgage the family home to buy into the partnership, and bank finance will play a large part in the deal. The incoming partner could be a corporation (corporate partner) or even a trust, which could be a partner. They would usually have their own cash available or raise bank finance to become a partner, if there were no restrictions and it was allowable.

The position where the partnership is sold as a whole to another partnership (or merger) is slightly different. All of the purchasing partners would agree with the selling partnership as to the deal to be done, in this case. Purchase or merger costs are usually met through internal resources (capital accounts or reserves) or bank finance.

If a sole trader

The sole trader will be selling his business as a going concern. This could be to a competitor, another person, a partnership or a company. The question is what is actually being sold, as the sole trader does not have shares, but may have hard assets and goodwill. The bank accounts of the sole trader are his own, and are unlikely to be included in the deal. Often the sole trader needs to incorporate first, so that a new and clean company is the object of the sale.

The sole trader purchasing a business would use bank finance, his own resources, and borrowings to finance the sale.

To make selling the business easier, the company could qualify under the enterprise investment scheme as an EIS qualifying company. Private investors could get tax reliefs for investing into the company at 30% of the investment made (50% if under the new SEEDEIS of up to £100,000 per person – but only CGT reliefs are available in 2013/14 unless backdating income tax relief). This may suit a company that buys back its own shares (and cancels them) from an exiting shareholder and then issues new shares that qualify under the EIS.

The routes to finance could be difficult at certain times. Following the credit crunch in 2007 and onwards and the general shortage of bank finance, more innovative funding ideas are required to achieve the sale at the right price. There are banking experts and deal makers who can structure most types of deals, if the business proposition stacks up. If not, the business owner will have to rely on other methods, such as internal purchase arrangements with employees and management.

Business brokers can help to find possible suitors for the business and put deals together for you. Finding someone, or an organisation to buy your business or shares when you wish to sell them, can be difficult - if doing it on your own. It is always better to use a third party negotiator if possible, not only to obtain the best price for the seller, but also to deal with the issues confidentially, especially if you do not wish to alert competitors at an early stage.

Constructing the sale efficiently will be of prime importance. The last thing you want is a massive tax bill, or being burdened with debt and difficult covenants, and this is why proper planning is most important.

Amongst other considerations, you may wish to consider all alternatives, including the use of pension schemes, spouse payments, trusts, offshore arrangements and other considerations. You may wish to retire abroad. It may be better to establish yourself abroad for a period, before making the sale, as this could have tax advantages.

22

Exiting the Business Successfully

Planning is the key word. You can plan to exit the business at retirement, or before retirement, or have plans in place should you be forced to exit the business through death or disability.

A number of key features and factors needed to be considered and taken into account.

Firstly, you considered your personal and business objectives. Then you constructed your business plan with business building blocks as to where you are now and where you wish to be in the future. You decided on a point of sale, and worked backwards to see what you had to accomplish to get there. You have developed a growth strategy over the next 3, 5 or ten years and will implement it.

You noted the importance of identifying, motivating and training successors to take over from you or key people that would be leaders in your organisation in the future. You identified, at an early stage, possible exit routes, and who the possible buyers and sellers might be. You have teed up likely purchasers of the business, and looked into how the purchase of the business would be facilitated, through finance externally, or through using employees and management internally.

You fully understand the numbers and know how to increase profits and reduce costs and taxation. You have undertaken a risk protection audit and tightened controls in your business, and arranged the necessary business protections required by the business. You have realised that what you have to sell is a business, not merely a profession or a job.

You have decided on strategies to improve sales, cash flow and profits, and even if you did not sell the business, you have a better business. You understand business life- cycle planning, and believe you know the best time to exit the business. The prospective purchaser has also studied the figures and believes this is the right time to buy.

You have spent a lot of time in improving the position of the business, and have adopted a business valuation method consistent with your industry sector, and one that is reasonable. You have learned how to add value, so that the share price of your business will be higher, thus demanding a higher price. You know exactly what you are selling, be it shares, property, goodwill or clients and the income streams generated to give the investor a return for his money.

You have prepared you your customers, employees and others for the sale. (so as not to lose them). Where employees are concerned, they are a happy and contented workforce, with prospects and career paths, and comparable employee benefits. They will continue to perform at the highest possible levels for the business, realising the more successful it is, the more successful they will be.

You know that your efforts, through thorough investigation and analysis, and preparation will enhance the sale price of your business by at least 30%.

The above is almost a lengthy mission statement for the successful business exit and succession plan. I make no apologies for it. The amount of planning and preparation work required is enormous, and doesn't happen overnight. It can be tackled in bite-sized chunks, and should not appear too daunting – as every really successful business person will tell you, the things that have to be done make commercial sense, and should be done, whether preparing the business for sale, or staying in it.

This book provides a number of areas where checklists can be made and implemented into any business. This is, in any event, a useful due diligence exercise.

Part 3

Wealth Creation

23

Using the Business for Wealth Creation

The business can be a source of wealth creation for the business owners as well as its employees. Business owners create wealth through successfully adding to profits year on year, they take out wealth to benefit themselves personally through dividends, income from the business and benefits. Ultimately the business may be sold and significant wealth creation occurs at that point.

Employees also use the business to create wealth. They can invest their income, and business benefits that come to them can enhance their wealth creation through pension schemes, shares, and other benefits.

The business can create surplus net income for the employee, thus increasing their potential for wealth creation, through having lower-costed group schemes for protection, health, disability and other insurances. If the employee was to pay for these benefits himself, the costs may be up to 15 times higher than if the company did it on a group scheme basis.

It is important to understand how a business creates profits. There are a number of different points of view on the treatment of 'profits', mainly dependant upon the structure and size of the business. Even the word 'profits' is not all it seems. Most people associate it with purely with cash surplus in the business that can be distributed to the business owners. However, 'profit' is not cash. Its measurement is determined by accounting conventions, some of which have nothing to do with cash flow. An example is depreciation, which is charged on property and plant, and reduces profit.

In this chapter, though, 'profit' is treated as the amount the business has, after paying tax, for distribution to the business owners or to be retained by the business. However this has a cost – a tax cost. To pay a dividend, the company must first pay tax on its profits. To take excess cash out of a partnership or LLP, tax must first be paid by the partners or members, and a sole trader will pay tax on money accruing in excess of deductible expenditure. The strategies which follow will concentrate on two distinct aspects. Firstly, how to reduce the incidences of taxation, which inevitably involves expenditure of some kind, and thereby increases profit. Secondly, how to distribute profits in the most efficient manner, or how best to use the profits to build wealth.

As profits are taxable, it actually costs the business money to be profitable. Therefore, one must seek the most efficient way to get money of the business or use it within business.

Understand the business cycle of profits

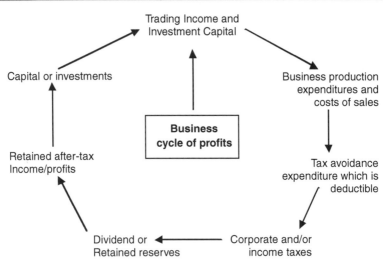

Trading Income and
Investment Capital

Capital or investments

Business production
expenditures and
costs of sales

**Business
cycle of profits**

Retained after-tax
Income/profits

Tax avoidance
expenditure which is
deductible

Dividend or ◄――――― Corporate and/or
Retained reserves   income taxes

At any point on this cycle, financial and corporate decisions can be made by managers or business owners to increase or decrease the incidence of profits and its distribution or retention.

Some of these can be pressure points where specific actions are initiated. For example, making pension contributions is a tax avoidance measure which reduces profits and therefore reduces taxation. It thus reduces the amount available for dividends or retained after-tax income, which may leave less capital for investment in sales generation. Each action will have some form of alternative counter-action or effect.

Your goals for building wealth through the business

Different perspectives can be translated into business goals. These will differ, depending upon the structure and size of the business.

Sole Trader

He or she is the business, if the business fails, losses are borne by the sole trader business owner, personally. It may even mean the loss of further personal assets, secured against loans for the business.

Success in business, however, brings its own rewards. The sole trader will endeavour to build wealth as far as possible. He or she will seek to reduce taxation and to maximise income.

There is no question of retaining high levels of after-tax-income in the business – it cannot be done, because of the personal nature of the business undertaking. If the business needs more cash, the business owner provides it. Although separate bank accounts are kept for personal and business needs, their ownership rests in the business owner personally. The sale of the business would be difficult – the business owner is the business, especially if he or she has not replicated themselves. On death, the best which could be hoped for is a sale of business assets – often at a 'fire sale value'.

The perspective of the sole trader therefore focuses on tax-efficient measures to reduce taxes payable and build personal wealth, which is itself protected.

Partnerships and LLP Members

Partners and LLP Members share in profits and liabilities equally, or in proportion to their partnership shares, or by agreement. Essentially, though, a partnership is by far the most vulnerable business structure because each partner is jointly and severally liable for the business debts of the partners and the partnership. This liability cab be restricted if the partnership incorporates. LLP's are less vulnerable as they have limited liability.

Partners are even more vulnerable because very few firms structure their partnership agreements properly. A partner may work for 40 years, building up his or her capital account in the business, only to find that the partnership cannot afford to pay out its value, on retirement in full (usually by instalments) or even on death, because it requires the cash for working capital. Profits in a partnership are apportioned as income to each partner and then taxed in that partner's hands. Partners and LLP members are taxed separately, with individual assessments raised, rather than on the firm. Individual partners are not jointly and severally liable for the total amount of tax payable by the partners. Partners are taxed under self-assessment, except for a salaried partner, taxed under PAYE.

The traditional perspective has been for partners to build up their capital accounts in the business (capitalised income not taken as drawings) which then accrue for their wealth-building. Capital accounts will only accrue after tax. This means that partners will give attention to tax-efficiency planning within the partnership itself. In addition, personal tax avoidance planning will be used to reduce the incidence of taxation and the building of personal wealth.

Partners manage the partnership assets for their own benefit and those of the other partners ultimately. Their overall perspective on profits will be the greatest accumulation of their capital accounts possible. However, problems could occur with transferring wealth on retirement or death.

At normal retirement date, the partners should consider either retiring or staying on in the partnership.

The Company

The business owners of a company are its shareholders. However, they may not (if they have smaller shareholdings or are passive investors) be able to influence company policy on how it operates, having to take advice from management on what is best for the company. However, the assumption is made here of a smaller business with shareholders active or reasonably close to the business. Companies are not as vulnerable as sole traders or partnerships. Shareholders are not responsible for the business debts – only the business is. However, their capital and therefore their wealth is at risk.

The return to shareholder is in the form of increasing capital values of their shares, as well as the expectation of dividends as an income flow. Therefore, the perspective of the shareholders is mostly retained profits to increase share values and dividends (from after-tax income) to increase income. This may be at odds with management who do not own shares, who would wish to build wealth through pre-tax avoidance schemes and increasing income. However, assuming that shareholders are also management, this allows a perspective of getting profits out of the business in the most tax-efficient manner, whilst enabling the business to continue as a powerhouse of ongoing wealth-creation. Taking out too much could affect cash flows and working capital, as well as capital creation through retained reserves, which in turn affects the stability of the business. They will therefore focus on tax reduction strategies, optimising profits and a dividend policy of tax-efficiency.

24

Profit Strategies for Sole Traders

Make maximum use of business deductions, allowable expenses and capital allowances

Claim the maximum deduction for business expenditure, allowable by law. Make sure that full expenditures incurred in using the home and personal or recreational assets in the business are claimed for. This will have the effect of reducing taxable income and therefore tax payable. Use the strategies to build personal asset wealth through the business.

Introduce your spouse or civil partner or partner, or the family members, into the business

You can introduce family members to the business to spread income, reduce taxes and use up personal allowances. You may pay family members who are employees a commercially justifiable salary, provide them with a car and make payments into a pension scheme for them. Taking family members into partnership may be a logical extension for your business objectives and can give more flexibility in the allocation of profits. It is also a useful succession planning tool. Bringing in family members (or others) will allow the business to continue if you die or retire. Spreading the load and 'keeping it in the family' is a justifiable way to create new taxpayers and more income tax-free. One of the best ways to increase family disposable income is by spreading taxable income to make use of personal allowances which every taxpayer has.

Example
Net profits earned by Stan Hinds this tax year will be £30,000. He employs his spouse Mary in the business at £10,000 and he takes out £20,000.

The position for Stan only:

Profits	£30,000
Less personal allowance	£9,440
	£20,560
Tax payable: 20% x £20,560 =	£4,112
Balance: net disposable income =	£25,888
(30,000 − 4,112)	

The joint position for Stan and Mary:

Stan		Mary
20,000	Profits/ Salary	10,000
9,440	Allowances	9,440
10,560	Taxable	560
(2,112)	Tax	(112)
£17,888	Disposable Balance	£9,888

Combined tax: £2,224 (a saving of £1,888) or 45.9% saving increase through less tax. Increase in disposable income: £2,224 for both of them together.

Increase pension funding to further reduce taxation and build wealth

Pension contributions will further reduce taxable income and enable the sole trader to invest in one of the most tax-efficient investments available – a pension fund. The fund itself is not taxed and grows tax-free. If you use the spread of taxpayers in the last strategy, the taxman can fund your pension contribution – at no cost to you! In fact, cash generated can now be used for further tax deductions/enhancements.

Example

Stan is now a 20% taxpayer as is Mary. Both contribute a total of £1,888 to personal pension schemes.

HMRC uplift through using the tax saved: 20% x £1,888 = £377.60 extra pension.

In fact both Stan and Mary should maximise their pension provision if possible, not only using other tax savings, but also other available 'net relevant earnings'. If Mary was an employee, or a partner, then she could have a minimum pension contribution of 100% of taxable income (in this case £10,000) or £3,600 (whichever is the greater) into a personal pension plan. There will be savings on National Insurance contributions for the business (as there are no NICs on pension contributions), and the HMRC will contribute 20% if she makes the contribution.

Make full use of personal investment and other tax deductions

Apart from pension funding, the sole trader can invest in EIS (Enterprise Investment Scheme – maximum investment is £1 million per person with 30% income tax relief) or VCT (Venture Capital Trust – £200,000 per person p.a.

with 30% income tax relief) schemes – a £100,000 investment gives £30,000 tax relief off an actual tax liability for EIS and £30,000 for VCT's. The EIS is a particularly relevant option if wishing to roll-over a capital gain and defer capital gains tax. We also have the new SEEDEIS with 50% tax relief up to £100,000 on capital gains tax only. Another tax deductible investment is the BPRA (Business Premises Renovation Allowance) where up to 100% deduction is available from taxable income. Both of these investments should be considered high risk. There are no other investments which are tax deductible or give relief from tax, apart from pensions. If a higher or additional rated taxpayer, additional relief is available for pensions' contributions at 20%-25% – claimable through your tax return.

Invest (profits) after-tax income wisely to build up personal wealth

Once the sole trader has readjusted his or her tax-planning for maximum efficiency and made whatever pre-tax deduction and investment arrangements are appropriate, investments are made from after-tax income. In other words, profits, having been taxed, are then allocated to investments (if not spent), according to the risk profile of the sole trader investor. Some capital is held back or allocated for further business development, invested in property and premises, and used in the business. This is translated into a base for further wealth, or to sell the business eventually for a significant gain.

25

Profit Strategies for Partners and LLP Members

Some of the profit-taking strategies for sole traders apply equally to partners and LLP members and will not be repeated here. These are in respect of:

- Making full use of business deductions, allowable expenses and capital allowances.
- If possible using the spouse, partner or civil partner in the business.
- Increasing pension funding to reduce taxation and build wealth.
- Making full use of personal investment and other tax deductions.
- Investing after-tax income wisely to build up personal wealth.

The following strategies apply more specifically to partnerships and partners (and LLP members) in maximising their profits.

Reorganise partnership and LLP borrowings to get maximum relief on interest payments

- Either the partners themselves arrange for substitute loans, claiming 100% of the interest as a deduction for providing finance to the firm or to increase partnership capital; and/or
- Restructuring of financing takes place, and/or
- Cash flow planning is undertaken, especially for firms with large loans or overdrafts.

Organise tax planning around partnership/LLP capital accounts to maximise and preserve wealth

Partnerships in England and Wales are not legal persona as they are in Scotland. In England and Wales, it is the individual members of a partnership who are trading and not the partnership itself. Partners and LLP members are directly assessed for income tax purposes. Once partnership expenditures and allowances are deducted from trading income, then the whole of business profits are treated as the partners' income and taxed under self assessment.

If there is a partnership agreement which stipulates how much the partner may draw down for personal use, this is strictly adhered to, with the balance of after-tax profits being loaned to the business by the partner. This is called the capital account and is largely used to fund working capital and capital expenditure. The interaction between the partner and business is therefore far greater than that between the shareholder and the company, for example.

The partnership is largely then valued on the basis of the combined value of these capital accounts and goodwill. The word 'goodwill' arises from the future value of expected income from probate and executors' fees on wills held by solicitors' practices. They were valued on the worth of their value – in that case 'goodwills'. It has therefore come into common parlance as the invisible future value of the business. Some partnerships specifically exclude goodwill from their partnership agreements – others have a formula for determining what it is. In the main, though, the value of each partner's share will be determined by the value of his or her loan account in the business – the capital account. The only problem is that partners bind themselves by agreement on how and when to take out their capital accounts. Often agreements will state that on retirement or death or leaving the firm, the capital account will be paid in instalments, with or without interest.

This is because the partnership:

*   Has not sufficient other capital to suffer a large reduction in capital at once – working capital will suffer.
*   Has not provided for the fact that at some time capital will be withdrawn.
*   Has not provided partnership protection policies to ensure immediate payouts in the event of death or disability.

This practice can have a disastrous effect on the wealth-building of the individual partner. His death could occasion the termination of the partnership or even result in bankruptcy – as could his retirement. There is an additional burden on the remaining partners, who now have one less fee earner, to increase earnings to pay out the leaving partner. Some just give it up. Quite frankly, the capital of the leaving partner is at great risk and his or her strategy must be to ensure payment of it as soon as possible. The strategy of the partnership should be:

*   Replace capital accounts for leavers with bank financing; and/or
*   Create a savings fund where a percentage of profits is invested each year, to contribute a leaver's capital; and/or
*   Create forms of alternative payments, and retain the capital account.

In connection with the above, some partnerships have a policy of maximum pension contributions. The retiring partner leaves his capital account behind, substituting the tax-free cash lump from his personal pension plan, SIPP or

SSAS arrangement for it. In addition, he receives a pension. As partnership profits are generated by the whole firm, of which the partner is a member, it is akin to the profits of a company in some ways. Value is reflected in compound growth pension funding instead of shares in this case.

A little known fact is that, in the absence of any agreement to contrary, the heirs of a deceased partner have an immediate call for cash from the partnership on the death of the partner. This cash call is for partnership value. Partners must, therefore, have partnership protection insurance to protect the partnership and its assets. To maximise personal wealth, the partner should make use of other personal investment and tax-reducing strategies. Partners remaining in the firm can also pay out an unfunded pension and lump sum, which is deductible to them individually. This strategy may offset the continued retention of the capital account, the repayment of which has no tax reliefs attaching to it.

Tax planning around partnership losses to preserve partners' wealth

In general, losses may be carried back and set off against other incomes, or the partner will have the choice of setting losses off against income in the year of the loss, or against income of the following year, or to carry losses forward to offset against trading income in future years. Your strategy is to take loss relief in a year when subject to higher rates of tax, rather than in low income years. Note that on the death or retirement of a partner, losses which have not been relieved cannot be carried forward. However, the carry-back of terminal losses may apply. Proper tax planning is most important to make full use of what is available to reduce taxes and build wealth.

If you contributed too much partnership capital, get paid interest

Interest paid to a partner on his own capital by the partnership is not an allowable expense, but an allocation of profit. However, payments made beyond the agreed amount of contributed capital are entitled to interest at 5% p.a. [Partnership Act 1890, s 24(3)]. This is an allowable expense to the partnership but taxable in the receiving partner's hands.

Make sure that excess allowances over tax due on partnership share is set off against other income

Any excess allowances over tax due on a partner's share of taxable profits can be set against any other income that the partner might have.

Maximise pension contributions as repayment of capital accounts may be slow

As mentioned previously, if the circumstances (and previous history of the firm) are such that slow repayments of capital accounts occur, then each partner either changes the system or makes maximum provision himself for tax deductible pension funding. Pension funding is the major method of building personal wealth outside the business, and of taking out pre-tax profits, so to speak, in the form of pension contributions.

Pay unfunded pensions and cash lump sums to retiring partners

Partners who usually postpone pension decisions due to a lack of structure or urgency should consider the following. Payment of a pension may be made from the profits of the continuing partners. Partners will therefore only face the expense of pension provision at actual retirement. This enables them to:

- Maximise capital in the business
- Find new partners to shoulder the burden
- Cope with retirement partners' needs

The partnership can pay a pension to retiring partners. This will be deductible to the remaining partners in their partnership proportions. To qualify as earned income for allowances, the pension must:

- Be paid in accordance with the partnership agreement or supplementary agreement.
- Not exceed 50% of the average profit of the retiring partner for the best three of the last seven years before retirement.
- Allow a tax-free cash sum of 25% of the notional accumulated sum to be taken.
- Be allowed to increase and/or be paid to a spouse or dependant.
- Be paid direct or by the purchase of an annuity.

Such a 'fund' may be used for the benefit of a partnership. No loans are allowed if a fund is established, but the scheme can purchase commercial property from the partnership and lease it back on commercial terms. Partners may therefore provide for pensions in a tax-efficient manner without having to set aside capital. The unfunded scheme has its limitations, especially where profits fluctuate, and pensions will probably be lower than if conventionally funded. It should not be relied upon as capital may not be available at the exact time when it is required.

Build up an investment fund to pay out capital accounts or pensions

The problem with partnership agreements and the fact that capital accounts are mainly used for working capital in the business (usually with the payment of no interest), lead to greater problems on death or retirement.

At a critical time, when the business needs the capital account money the most, it may have to give it up. In fact, under the **1890 Partnership Act**, heirs on death have an immediate call for cash (unless other arrangements are made) and this could cripple the business.

The best solutions are:

* A savings fund to pay out retiring or deceased partners.
* A phased payment plan, say beginning five years before retirement of the capital account – possibly to boost pension funding.
* Maximum pension funding – or the partners pay a lump sum and unfunded pension to the retired partner or his dependants (and the firm keeps the capital account for a longer period)
* Staying on as a partner and dying 'in harness' so as to maximise business property reliefs on death.

Partners' and LLP Members' wealth is often at great risk left in the partnership or LLP. If bank finance can be exchanged for personal capital, then do it.

26

Profit Strategies for Companies

Depending on the business objectives and management policies of the company, taking the needs of the shareholders as well as the strength, well-being and status of the company, into account, it will:

* Endeavour to make best use of tax reducing strategies pre-profit taking; and
* Decide on the best wealth-creation terms for shareholders.

Usually there is a conflict between these two objectives. Most tax- reducing strategies involve expenditure of one kind or another. Expenditure which is allowable against taxable income will ultimately reduce the amount available for shareholders by way of dividends. For most closely-connected companies, this does not pose a problem, as the shareholders are usually its directors. For large companies with more shareholders, some of them unconnected, the company will formulate a dividend policy commensurate with the stage of the business growth it is in. In the final analysis, it comes down to a sensible balance or mix. The directors would want to retain sufficient capital for capitalisation and working capital needs, now and in the future. At the same time, they would wish to maximise their personal wealth either through:

* Increasing value of their shares or share options (if they have them)
* Dividends
* Bonuses
* Other wealth-creation plans funded by the business, such as pensions and employee benefits.

The main challenge, having decided on business planning policy, will be the allocation of pre-tax profits to funding internal schemes and cash flows, and the allocation of post-tax profits to dividends and retain retained reserves.

Paying dividends or bonuses – decide which is the best route

The Taxes Act 1988, s 834(3) has dividends taxable in the year in which they fall due for payment. A dividend from a UK company carries a tax credit [TA 1988, section 231; FA 1993, section 78]. The tax-credit available to those receiving dividends is restricted to 10%. Thus a dividend of £90 is treated as gross income of £100. Individuals receiving dividends, who are liable for tax at 40%, will have to pay an additional 22.5%% on dividend income (if a 45% taxpayer, the additional tax is 27.5%). If an individual is not subject to higher rate tax, the 10% tax credit is deemed sufficient. At present, this represents a saving of 50% on the basic rate of 20%. Other taxable income is always taxed first in the hierarchy and then dividend income. Income (including savings income) is taxed as follows in 2013/14:

- At 20% on the first £34,370.
- At 40% on the balance over the basic rate threshold to £150,000
- At 50% over £150,000

Dividends for basic rate taxpayers are taxed at 10%, (covered by the tax credit of 10%) and for 40% higher rate taxpayers at 32.5%, and 45% additional rate taxpayers at 37.5%.

There are various levels of tax efficiency in deciding whether executives should take bonuses or receive dividends. Likewise, for the company, it may be more economical to pay bonuses rather than dividends as a form of wealth extraction, for example, for profits at any level of corporation taxation, it is more economic to pay dividends than bonuses. One should consider the effect of regular dividend payments on share values. Probably it would be better to have different classes of shares which have different dividend entitlements.

Corporation Tax Rates in 2013/14
- On Profits £0-300,000 is   20%
- £300,001-1,500,000 is   23.75%
- £1,500,001 and over is   23%

Dividends versus bonus – net effect 2013/14

Assume the trading profit in the company was £100,000. This could be paid by way of bonus, dividends, or both. At different levels of corporation tax it may be better to take a dividend rather than a bonus and vice versa. The director is a 40% income taxpayer. No dividends fall into the basic rate band.

Bonus route

Bonus (£100,000 less employer NICs)	£87,873
(Employer NICs 13.8%	12,127)
Employee NICs at 2%	1,757
Tax at 40%	35,149
Net to Director	**£50,967**

Dividend route

At 20% corporation tax

Profits	£100,000
Corporation tax	£20,000
Balance for distribution (with tax credit)	£80,000
Higher rate taxpayer director at 32.5%	£26,000
Net to Director	**£54,000**

At 23.75% corporation tax

Profits	£100,000
Corporation tax	£23,750
Balance for distribution (with tax credit)	£76,250
Higher rate taxpayer director at 32.5%	£24,781
Net to Director	**£51,469**

At 23% corporation tax

Profits	£100,000
Corporation tax	£23,000
Balance for distribution (with tax credit)	£77,000
Higher rate taxpayer director at 32.5%	£25,025
Net to Director	**£51,975**

Summary

The company has £100,000 to spend as a bonus or a dividend. The net effect, after tax, is as follows:

Bonus to director	£50,967
Dividend – 20% tax company	£54,000
Dividend – 23.75% tax company	£51,469
Dividend – 24% tax company	£51,975

As the table shows, the director is better off taking the dividends in all cases.

If a combined bonus and a pension contribution was made for the director, allocating £50,000 of trading profit to each, the position would be as follows:

Bonus route + Pension Contribution

Bonus (£50,000 less employer NICs)	£43,937
(Employer NICs 13.8%	6,063)
Employee NICs at 2%	879
Tax at 40%	17,575
Available cash	25,483
Pension Contribution	50,000
Net to director	**£75,463**

Improve the position of the director by making a pre-tax pension contribution for him

The company will still spend a total of £100,000 made up of bonus, employer's NIC on the bonus, employee's NIC and the pension contribution. The net position for the executive is £75,463, made up of bonus after tax plus pension. (The company also saves further NIC through the reduced bonus.)

The bonus/pension split in value or wealth-creation terms is considerably better than the bonus alone or any of the dividend positions. It also largely overcomes the problem of reinvestment of the bonus or dividends, as the pension route (for part of package) provides a tax-efficient investment medium.

Make use of other NIC avoidance schemes to reduce taxation

The business may wish to benefit executives by diverting bonuses or salary increases into schemes which avoid National Insurance contributions payable by the company. Whilst the HMRC do their utmost to outlaw these schemes through new legislation (the latest attack has been to have every proposed scheme declared in advance). Salary sacrifice is allowable, and some schemes have only the interest element taxable at the official rate of tax.

You can do anything legal to AVOID tax, but don't do anything to EVADE it.

Take out investigation insurance policies if utilising avoidance schemes

The chances are the company may at some stage (in any event, whether avoiding tax or not) come under intensive investigation from the DWP (for NIC), from HM Customs and Excise (for VAT) and from the HMRC (for taxes), and this can be a very costly event. Cheap investigations insurance cover is available from about £150 a year and covers the costs of investigations up to say, £60,000 worth of fees.

Utilise all personal allowances and reliefs to reduce taxes

You build personal wealth from what you retain, not what you have to give away in taxes.

Make sure the business is deducting all it can in capital allowances and business expenditures

Bigger deductions give rise to bigger profits, so the company or business should regularly carry out internal checks and audits as well as credit management controls.

Borrow from a director's pension fund rather than a bank

Interest payable to the pension fund is tax deductible to the company. Interest paid to the pension fund accumulates free of all taxes. This is an important strategy to increase wealth and to keep the cycle of financing 'within the business' alive. Loans are available from SIPP and SSAS arrangements at up to 50% of the value of scheme assets.

Invest retained profits wisely

Retained profits are after-tax profits held as reserves in the company and capitalised. They are also a measure of wealth in the company, available for distribution on liquidation (to creditors, then shareholders). The value of the balance sheet and subsequent shareholders' value is increased if profits are retained in this way. Many companies have idle cash balances not earning any interest (or negligible amounts), some millions of pounds being on call, but never called upon. The answer is to have a proper investment policy for growth or income or property purchases for excess cash.

Sell shares and retain wealth by using capital gains tax exemptions

Ultimately the shareholder will wish to sell shares in the company or pass them on to future generations for dividend flow or subsequent sale. There are capital gains tax reliefs and business property reliefs available on retirement, sale of shares or on death. This allows you to maximise your wealth position without paying additional taxes. In some circumstances, the company may have to set up specific exit routes for shareholders – in other words, make their shares more marketable. This is accomplished internally through employee share trust arrangements and other share purchase and share option schemes, and externally via the Alternative Investment Market (AIM), the Stock Exchange or sales to private investors.

From the above, you have seen that profits may be taken out of business on a pre-tax basis or after-tax; pre-tax involves the use of wealth-builders, such as pension schemes; the different choices for when to take dividends or bonuses are given; after-tax means using dividends, if a company, or intensive personal financial planning if a sole trader, partner or member of an LLP for investment purposes; the question of whether to leave profits in the business to add value can only occur after tax.

Investments and tax shelters

Once the business has begun creating wealth, it must then develop investment strategies to harness it and preserve it. It is no good at all if the business fails to use what it makes to provide a better financial future for itself and its owners. Wealth-retention and creation through the business is the ultimate objective of the business owners and shareholders personally. Internal investments will add to the strengths of the business itself, whilst external investments via the people in the business will increase their wealth personally. Internal investments are those made by the business; external investments are those made by or for the business owners and employees.

Wealth accumulation

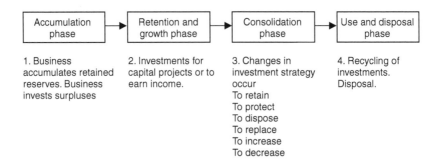

Accumulation phase	Retention and growth phase	Consolidation phase	Use and disposal phase
1. Business accumulates retained reserves. Business invests surpluses	2. Investments for capital projects or to earn income.	3. Changes in investment strategy occur To retain To protect To dispose To replace To increase To decrease	4. Recycling of investments. Disposal.

Determine the investment policy of the business and its attitude to risk

Usually the investment policy of the business is determined according to which phase of the business growth cycle it finds itself in.

Business growth cycle and investment policy

The business growth cycle shows the business attitude to risk and capital at various stages of the development cycle, the link to surpluses and the investment policy in respect of the these surpluses:

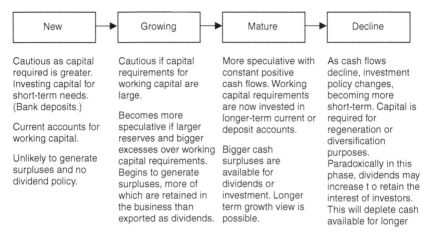

New	Growing	Mature	Decline

Cautious as capital required is greater. Investing capital for short-term needs. (Bank deposits.)

Current accounts for working capital.

Unlikely to generate surpluses and no dividend policy.

Cautious if capital requirements for working capital are large.

Becomes more speculative if larger reserves and bigger excesses over working capital requirements. Begins to generate surpluses, more of which are retained in the business than exported as dividends.

More speculative with constant positive cash flows. Working capital requirements are now invested in longer-term current or deposit accounts.

Bigger cash surpluses are available for dividends or investment. Longer term growth view is possible.

As cash flows decline, investment policy changes, becoming more short-term. Capital is required for regeneration or diversification purposes. Paradoxically in this phase, dividends may increase t o retain the interest of investors. This will deplete cash available for longer

Businesses with rapidly increasing cash surpluses will be actively looking for the best investment medium, whether for income generation or growth.

Determine the availability of investment resources

Capital and income for investments will usually come from the following sources:

- Shareholders' capital
- Directors' loan accounts
- (Partners and LLP capital accounts – for Partnerships and LLPs)
- Retained reserves from after-tax profits
- Cash from pre-tax surpluses or profits
- Unused portion of loans
- Sale of assets
- Investment income
- Divided income
- Dividend waivers
- Operating efficiencies and cost reduction exercises
- Windfalls, such as trade discounts and barter, payments on insurance policies (death of a key person)
- Tax, VAT and other repayments

Trading income should not be considered for investment purposes – only banked in short-term current accounts for future transfer to longer term deposit accounts if not required.

Determine the future expenditure of the business and its sources

Business expenditures should be calculated over at least a three to five year period – longer if significant capital expenditures are expected or planned. These expenditures are usually the following:

- Working capital expenditures – operating expenditure
- Employee benefit costs, such as pension contributions
- Administration and other fixed costs, computerisation
- Variable costs associated with production and sales processes, purchase of stock and raw materials
- Capital expenditures, such as plant and machinery
- Dividends and dividend policy
- Bonuses and commissions
- Legal, accounting and other fees
- Acquisition and merger costs
- Property acquisition costs

Expenditure items must be 'cash flowed' and their times and rate of expenditure noted. Investment policy and strategies can then be implemented for either short – medium or long – term investments. For example the business may wish to save for future capital expenditure rather than take out loans for it.

Link the business's investment strategy to tax shelter and tax deductible investments

The return on the investment increases significantly depending on its tax-efficiency.

Determine the best investment

Take into account the risk profile of the business, capital or income requirements, and need for growth and tax reliefs requirements.

As a general rule, lower risk investments with 'guaranteed capital' will have no growth and are usually income-producing. Higher-risk investments usually have capital at risk and therefore expect higher returns in respect of growth, with little or no income. The individual may wish to limit capital risk by having cash investment within a growth portfolio. Most people are concerned with the risk of loss of capital as opposed to the risk of what they may earn beating inflation in the long-term.

Select the most tax-efficient investments for surplus cash and invest in tax shelters

Once the business has decided on its investment strategy, in accordance with its business objectives, and made the necessary allocations for further expenditure (using short-term usually fixed interest investments), it can invest its surpluses by choosing a mix of investments. Some investments may even be protected from creditors (such as pensions – but only if there is no fraud). By investing in tax-sheltered investments, the investment begins tax efficiently and the shelter ensures its continuance. These types of investments are the best wealth builders.

Your best tax shelter is the business's pension fund. Maximise contributions to it

Contributions to pension funds are tax deductible to the business and to the higher rate taxpaying individual making allowable contributions. Once made, the contributions compound tax-free within the pension fund. The value of the contributions made is not taxed in hands of individual members of the fund. Nor are they taxed as a benefit in kind.

The company or employer does not pay NIC on contributions, saving 13.8% on cash flow.

If the business gets into trouble, the pension fund stands outside the business and is for the benefit of its members. Because the pension fund itself is not an asset of the business, it is not reflected on the balance sheet. (except for the liabilities of final salary – DB- schemes). However, its existence is known and this strengthens the profile of the business. The employer-owned scheme for directors or partners (SSAS) may be used as a source of funds (as can SIPPs which are individually owned). Loans are available to the business for commercial purposes. Loans taken by the business must have interest paid at a commercial rate. This interest is deductible to the business, but not taxed in the pension fund itself. The business can virtually set its own rate of growth in the fund at higher levels.

Pension funds in surplus could help the business's cash flow by taking contribution holidays – another example of their flexibility.

Use a pension scheme to protect the assets of the business

The business's property (premises) could be purchased from a third party (or connected persons) by the owner's pension scheme (SSAS or SIPP) and rented to the business. The trustees of the pension fund have wide powers and can take or make loans, arrange mortgages and so on. The rental income paid by the pension fund accrues free of all taxes in the pension fund, and is tax-deductible to the business. The pension fund is in effect a trust which is most flexible. Purely discretionary, it does not suffer tax charges like other trusts, nor does it have to cease after 80 years.

Property held this way may be utilised by future family members (so long as they participate in the business) for as long as there are future family generations. They simply become members of the pension fund. Business assets can therefore be protected within a pension fund. A SSAS can even purchase shares in the sponsoring company – usually up to 5% worth. The pension fund is your most tax-efficient tax shelter. Individuals in business (sole traders, partners and LLP members) may use a self-invested personal pension to hold property and other investments. On retirement, tax-free cash is payable to members. The pension itself is taxable once received.

Contribution limits are very high. You can contribute up to 100% of salary or 'relevant earnings', with a minimum of £3,600 gross (£2,880 net) if you have no earnings. Up to £50,000 can be contributed in this way in 2013/14, with a lifetime limit of £1.5 million in 2013/14.

The company or business may invest in other tax efficient investments such as EZTs

Any individual or business may invest in an Enterprise Zone Trust (EZT) investment, and obtain 100% tax relief on the buildings element, but not the land – the amount of the investment is unlimited, but long term.

The only problem is that EZT investments are fairly scarce, because EZT zones, where investments are made have filled up, leading to a shortage of investment opportunities.

Some Enterprise Zone Property Trusts or syndicates offer a pooled arrangement where investors share in the capital allowances related to the property. Investors would expect an income from the property investment (rental income of, say, 7%) as well as a capital gain. Unlimited investments may be made into BPRA that reduce taxable income.

A company may invest in an ESOT – an Employee Share Owner Trust, for tax shelter and working capital enhancements

Capital, either borrowed from a bank (or other source) or given by the company to the employee share trust (ESOT), is tax deductible to the company, once beneficial ownership occurs for the employee. The ESOT uses the cash to purchase shares in the company or from shareholders. If purchased from the company, the company receives cash which can be used as working capital, or invested elsewhere – for example into tax deductible pension contributions.

The ESOT is a tax shelter for employees, who take shares (which can be funded through profit – related pay schemes and bonuses) and receive dividends. However, it can be used as a store of wealth by the company. The ESOT can be used to funnel tax-efficient cash to the company. It can also be used as tax-deferral vehicle.

The business can make investments (usually in property, plant and machinery) for capital allowances

Capital allowances are another form of tax relief, but given in a different way. If the investment qualifies for capital allowances, then the capital cost of the investment is 'written off' or 'written down' for tax purposes, over a number of years, depending upon its HMRC-assessed life expectancy. For 2013/14 a 100% investment allowance will apply to the first £250,000 of expenditure on plant and machinery in the general plant and machinery pool. In 2013/14, the rate of writing down allowances on plant and machinery will be 8% for assets not qualifying for the annual investment allowance or first year allowance and 18% on other plant and machinery. Cars allowances are based on CO_2 emissions.

Invest in legitimate NIC avoidance schemes to build executive wealth

Tax avoidance is OK, tax evasion is not. Businesses or individuals may arrange their tax affairs in any legitimate way to avoid the payment of taxes. It is worth repeating the following words of Lord Clyde (in **Ayrshire Pullman Motor Services and Ritchie V IRC**) in relation to how the taxpayer may protect assets from the taxman:

'No man in this country is under the smallest obligation, moral or other, so to arrange his legal relations to his business or to his property as to enable the Inland Revenue to put the largest possible shovel into his stores. The Inland Revenue is not slow… to take every advantage which is open to it under the taxing statutes for the purpose of depleting the taxpayer's pocket. And the taxpayer is, in like manner, entitled to be astute to prevent, so far as he honestly can, the depletion of his means by the Revenue'.

Legitimate investments or bonus payments constructed in such a way as to avoid National Insurance contributions (NIC) and other taxes legitimately can be significant tax shelters for the business as well as employees.

The use of trusts, investments and specific modes of payments enable the individual to build wealth outside the business – tax efficiently. Some schemes avoid NIC, PIID benefits and other taxation – savings which can be utilised elsewhere by the business for investment purposes.

Get the best interest rates

Shop around for this – the high street banks are notorious for paying little to no interest on bank accounts for businesses. However, there are certain banks that will pay slightly more. If you do not need funds for some time, one AA+

bank offers a guaranteed deposit account that pays up to 14% p.a. as long as the investment is left for 5-6 years and for £250,000+. The account is in the business's name at all times. The interest can be ballooned to a payment date to suit the business for tax purposes.

Pay the best interest rates for loan account money

Any director, partner or LLP member leaving his director's or partner's or LLP member's loan account to lie fallow in the business is making a poor investment decision. Granted, it may be spare capital, but directors may also have borrowed the money in the first place to lend it to the business. He or she may even be paying (albeit deductible) interest on the money borrowed, but loan account money will always be dead money to the director, partner, LLP member. It will never grow, as it is not invested, only loaned. An amount of £50,000 loaned to a business 30 years ago is still only worth £50,000 (less in value for inflation). The opportunity cost lost could be 30 year x 6% compound growth on £50,000 = £287,174; This position is made even worse if no interest is payable.

If a director is in for the long term and wants his money in the business, it may be better to put it in as equity, not loan capital. The level of risk is the same if the business goes down. However the upside of capital growth in shares and dividends may far outweigh the downside of low or no interest and no capital growth in a loan account.

A director's loan account is the worst possible long-term investment strategy for him – great for the business (to have free money) but bad for the director and his or her wealth – building programme. Replace it with bank finance if possible and allow the director to invest for growth. There are also inheritance tax issues for director loan accounts – they do not qualify for BPR and are taxable in your estate.

Review investment arrangements regularly – at least once a year

Regular reviews are essential to keep pace with changing business circumstances. For example, it is easy it was to allow review arrangements to slide with respect to investments within a pension scheme – the loss of end fund value over 18 years is 20% for a 1% investment loss of performance today.

Constantly review individual and business cost savings and investment strategies. By squeezing a bit here and a bit there, vast savings can be made. Once made, these should be judiciously invested for further growth or income for the business.

Help employees to build personal wealth. The 'knock-on' effect makes for wealthier businesses

Offering employee benefits, pension benefits, share options and schemes, profit-related pay and wealth-building arrangements to executives and employees – whether reward orientated or performance orientated – will tie the employee and his or her loyalty to the business. Performance – related schemes will improve the business's performance and wealth.

This really is a case of spending now to accumulate later. However, in many instances the business owners are the wealth – builders, and those who look after their people will have their people look after them.

It is easy to motivate company employees by giving them shares or share options in the company – but employees of a sole trader or partnership or LLP have no such structure. The answer is to build a 'phantom share scheme' using profit related performance pay and individual savings accounts (ISAs). A trust is set up for employees and the better the business does, the more it contributes a part of its profitability for its employees. It could give a taxable salary increase, but the motivating effects of that are soon lost. It is far better to build the 'Partnership Share Scheme' and for employees to be a part of that – better still as they will now be invested in the investment market, and their investment risk will be spread, which is not the case with investing in one business.

Business owners must invest their business's cash surpluses sensibly, whether in fixed interest or growth investments. It is important for the business to know where it is on the business wealth creation cycle and also its development cycle, as this determines its investment policies.

You have the choice to build the business and retain wealth within the business (to maximise it one day when the business is sold), or to diversify as much as possible, and build wealth outside the business as well as in it. Creating wealth for the business as well as the people in it are important jump-off points for succession planning. Do not be the one who says 'My business is my pension', because things may turn out differently and you could end up with neither pension nor business if you do not plan properly.

Part 4

Bringing your Succession Planning Strategies together

27

Conclusion

We have considered individual as well as business owner succession planning. These are not two separate planning areas. Individual succession and lifestyle planning will impact on the business, and business succession planning will impact on the individual, his family and heirs.

By bringing both individual and business streams together, we have a consolidated succession plan taking into account both personal and business objectives.

For example, a personal objective may be to fund pension contributions to have a successful retirement. The business objective is to provide for employee benefits, which include retirement benefits. The contributions will be deductible to the business, and will therefore reduce corporation tax, which in turn increases profits. The personal and business objectives are complementary.

A personal objective may be that the individual wishes to retire at age 55. The business objective is that the business owner intends to build value over the next 10 years, which will take her to age 57. Here, the objectives are similar, but have different timings attaching to them. As a result, the personal objective may have to be adjusted to the new retirement date.

The individual wishes to leave his shares to his heirs and bequeaths them to his children by writing a will. The business objective is to ensure that cash passes to the estate instead of shares (as the surviving shareholders do not want family members who are not involved in the business to hold shares on the death of a shareholder), and a double option agreement is drawn up with life assurance on each shareholder in a business trust to ensure this happens. The contractual business agreement takes precedence over the will. The will is therefore ineffectual for this part, and the individual needs to realign his personal objectives. His personal succession plan would have been to direct his shareholding to his children, and in the absence of the business agreement, this would have happened. However, here there is a conflict of objectives, and the business objective has prevailed.

There is therefore no rigid formula to go by. What the setting of goals and objectives for the business and for the individuals does, is to create a thought process, and an analysis of the present position, according to differing viewpoints. Through mediation and negotiation, the wishes of both parties can be achieved – well more or less so, depending on the circumstances.

What succession planning does is to open up debate on future scenarios and goals and how to best achieve them. It may be that shareholder A has taken professional advice on the tax implications of selling his shares and the best and most efficient way to retire from the business. None of the other shareholders have done this, and have set out their retirement and exit position in a different way, which is not very efficient. Shareholder A is able to convince them that his way is better, and this route is then adopted for all.

The ultimate objective

This would be:

- A comprehensive set of goals and objectives that coincide for all the business owners.
- This can then be developed into strategy and a policy is formulated for implementation.
- It causes intense focus on the business model and to get it right. A business plan is formulated taking into account the need for continuity, leadership and succession, within an infrastructure of growth and profitability.
- It provides for a protective framework to build the business without fear of loss.
- It creates wealth for both employees and business owners, as well as an enjoyable working environment that is performance driven.
- The needs of all parties are taken into account, across both individual and business objectives and requirements, and with a common purpose.
- There is a track to run on, where all of the bases have been covered.

In the final analysis, succession planning is not merely the identification of a successor or leader to take over the business, but also includes how best to leave the business, having created wealth in the process, and how to deal with issues arising on death, incapacity and retirement, and devolving assets for future generations.

Abbreviations

AIM	Alternative Investment market
APR	Agricultural Property relief
BPR	Business property Relief
BPRA	Business premises Renovation Allowance
BR19	State pension forecast form
CGT	Capital Gains Tax
CEO	Chief Executive Officer
CIC	Critical Illness Cover
DB	Defined Benefits pension scheme
DC	Defined Contribution pension scheme
EIS	Enterprise Investment scheme
EMI	Enterprise Management Incentive
EPS	Earnings per share
ESOT	Employee Share owner trust
EZ	Enterprise Zone
FA	Finance Act
HMRC	Her Majesty's Revenue and Customs
HR	Human resources
IHT	Inheritance Tax
ISA`	Individual Savings Account
LLP	Limited Liability Partnership
MBO/MBI	Management Buy Out/Buy In
MD	Managing Director
PET	Potential Exempt Transfer
PHI	Permanent Health Insurance
SEEDEIS	Seed enterprise investment scheme
SIPP	Self Invested Personal Pension
SSAS	Small Self Administered Scheme
TCGA	Taxation of Chargeable Gains Act 1992
VAT	Valued added Tax
VCT	Venture capital trust

Bibliography

Business Protection Simplified, Tony Granger (Management Books 2000)

Tolleys Tax Guide (LexisNexis)

Tolleys Practical tax newsletters/ Tax Service (LexisNexis)

Inheritance tax Simplified, Tony Granger (Management Books 2000)

Pensions Simplified, Tony Granger (Management Books 2000)

Personal Financial Planning Manual, Bently Jennison (Tottel)

Tolleys Tax Planning for Owner Managed Businesses (Lexisnexis)

Limited Liability Partnerships – A guide for Professionals, Paterson and Britton (Kings College, London)

Tax Efficient Investments Guide, Tony Granger (Mentor)

Tolleys Professional Partnership Handbook (LexisNexis)

Wealth Strategies for your Business, Tony Granger (Random House/ Century)

HMRC and other websites

Index

A

Advance decisions 27

B

Bank accounts 32
Bonuses 95
Business drivers 74
Business objectives 51
Business plan 53
Business Premises Renovation
   Allowance (BPRA) 111, 129,
   144
Business risk areas 81
Business sale 105
Buy-back (shares) 56

C

Capital allowances 145
Capital gains investments 113
Career paths 73
Care, long term 34
Civil partners 127
Continuing liabilities 103

D

Death 108
Death After Retirement 37
Death Before Retirement 36
Death planning 21
Deferred interest 113
Deposit accounts 113
Directors' loan accounts 101
Disability 41
Discounted cash flow 61
Divorce 42
Drawdown pension schemes 38
Due diligence 60

E

Early retirement 39
Employees 93, 96
Employee Share Owner Trusts 144
Employee Share Scheme trusts 93
Enterprise Management Incentive
   share option scheme (EMI) 94
Enterprise Zone Trusts (ETZ) 144
Estate planning 33
Exit routes 58

F

Free cashflow multiplier 65
Future expenditure 142
Future leaders 73

H

Health 41

I

Ill health 39, 41
Illness 86
Income protection 41, 87
Increasing business value 64
Inheritance tax 39
Intestacy 22
Intrinsic added value 65
Intrinsic value 62
Investment bonds 113
Investment fund 134
Investment management 146
Investments and savings 39

K

Keyman insurance 82

L

Lasting power of attorney (LPA) 27,
   35

Leadership 74
Life assurance 25
Life insurance 82
Liquidity 69
Living wills 27
Loan accounts 146
Long term care 34

M

Management Buy-in 55
Management Buy-out 55
Managers 93
Money purchase pension scheme
    38

N

Negotiation 67
Net assets 60
NIC avoidance schemes 145
Nil Rate Band 32

O

Objectives 49
Occupational pension scheme 37

P

Partial sale 56
Partnerships 125, 130
    retiring from 101
Pension contributions 111, 133
Pension fund 143
Pension funds 39
Pension schemes 143
    drawdown 38
    money purchase 38
    occupational 37
Personal allowances 114
Personal objectives 51
Price-earnings ratio 61
Profit margin 68
Property 39
    ownership 33

R

Rate of return 61
Retirement 104
Retirement planning 40
Return on owner's equity 69
Return on total assets 68
Risk protection 65

S

Sale of the business 105
SAYE schemes 95
SEEDEIS 111, 117
Share listing 56
Sole traders 103, 124, 127
    death 108
Spouses 127
Succession plan 51
Succession planning
    who is involved 77

T

Talent (in the business) 75
Tax deferred investments 112
Tax free investments 112
Tax planning 114
Tax reducing investments 111
Tax shelters 142
Time line, setting 57
Trade sale 55
Trusts 25, 93

U

Unfunded pensions 133

V

Valuation 62
Venture Capital 57

W

Wealth creation 123, 147
Wills 22, 23
    living 27

For further confidential information on succession planning, send this page to:

Business Strategies
11 Melbourne Rise
Bicton Heath
Shrewsbury
SY3 5DA

Name _____

Address

_____

_____

_____

_____

Postcode _____

Telephone: _____

Fax: _____

Email: _____

Post to the address above,
or email to tony@tonygranger.com

Please photocopy this page to avoid spoiling your book